Poverty and Wealth
in James

Poverty and Wealth
in James

Pedrito U. Maynard-Reid

ORBIS BOOKS

Maryknoll, New York 10545

The Catholic Foreign Mission Society of America (Maryknoll) recruits and trains people for overseas missionary service. Through Orbis Books Maryknoll aims to foster the international dialogue that is essential to mission. The books published, however, reflect the opinions of their authors and are not meant to represent the official position of the society.

© 1987 by Pedrito U. Maynard-Reid
Published by Orbis Books, Maryknoll, NY 10545
All rights reserved
Manufactured in the United States of America

Manuscript editor: William H. Schlau

Library of Congress Cataloging-in-Publication Data

Maynard-Reid, Pedrito U.
  Poverty and wealth in James.

  Bibliography: p.
  Includes index.
  1. Bible. N.T. James—Criticism, interpretation,
etc.   2. Poor—Biblical teaching.   3. Wealth—Biblical
teaching.   I. Title.
BS2785.2M32   1987   277'.91067   86-23506
ISBN 0-88344-417-8 (pbk.)

For Violet, my wife,
Pedrito II, my son,
and Natasha, my daughter,
without whom I am incomplete

Contents

INTRODUCTION   *1*

CHAPTER 1   *13*
Social Stratification in the First Century A.D.

CHAPTER 2   *24*
Poor and Rich in Jewish and Christian Literature
    The Old Testament Literature   25
    The Intertestamental Literature   28
    First-Century Jewish Life   30
    The New Testament Literature   32

CHAPTER 3   *38*
The Great Reversal: James 1:9–11

CHAPTER 4   *48*
Favoritism and the Poor: James 2:1–13

CHAPTER 5   *68*
The Merchant Class and the Poor: James 4:13–17

CHAPTER 6   *81*
The Rich Agriculturalists and the Poor: James 5:1–6

NOTES   *99*

INDEX   *133*

Introduction

METHODOLOGY

Studies on the Epistle of James have been primarily literary and theological in their orientation. Not much attention has been paid to the social milieu out of which the document arose and how the social ethos impinged upon the thought of the writer. Until the 1970s this provincialism and narrowness of perspective had for a long time dominated New Testament studies in general. It was in the 1960s that a response began to develop and took the form of a growing discontent with exegetical and theological models used in New Testmament interpretation. The hermeneutic discussion of the 1960s was designed to appeal only to a certain level of scholars. Even the answers given to questions raised by such systems as Form and Redaction Criticism regarding the social context of individual New Testament documents were unsatisfactory to many biblical students. Many times those systems distorted the historical realities of the community out of which the document arose because their focus was primarily theological and very little social.[1]

In the 1970s and 1980s the social context of the New Testament has been and is attracting the attention of scholars. Because this area of study has a more concrete base than other approaches, it has infused new life into the study of New Testament Christianity and is presently exercising a revolutionary effect on New Testament scholarship.

In order to grasp even partially the identity and concern of the community of James and to come to grips with the intent of the author, we must move beyond the language of the document and the logic of the beliefs of the community. We must address the issue of the community's social existence and how theological beliefs functioned within that existence. Only thus can we be faithful to the totality of the message of the document.[2]

The question of a satisfactory method for a study of the social milieu of the New Testament as a whole and individual documents like James arises at this point. Various theories and models are currently being proposed. These present numerous possibilities, as well as some confusion. They also raise some vital questions.

First of all, where do we begin a social reconstruction of early Christianity or of a particular community? What are the sources for this reconstruction? We have available to us literary (biblical and nonbiblical), archeological, and culturo-geographical data, as well as modern sociological and anthropological theories. All these sources are indispensable if a holistic conceptualization of the social reality of the New Testament is to be realized.

Where then shall we begin? With modern sociological theories and models? With literary sources outside the New Testament? While we may expect to gain insights from the theories and sources, neither of those two options seems to be the best initial route to follow because both are external to the text and tend to bring to bear on it presuppositions and conclusions that are extraneous to the intent of the text. We must begin with the New Testament itself and there break the ground of understanding. It must be allowed to speak for itself. And this can be done only by the exegetical enterprise. We must agree, therefore, with Abraham Malherbe's suggestion that the sources with which we should be primarily concerned are the New Testament documents. Here we must begin, and "we must read them with a sensibility to their social dimensions before we hasten to draw larger patterns."[3] In addition, we should note not only their social dimensions per se, but a social dimension which is encased in theological and pastoral concerns.[4]

All this is not to deny the viability of using models from the social sciences. Most of the work that has been done in the social aspect of the New Testament has gone the route of sociological theories.[5] A number of articles have been written on this method of approach,[6] and a number of studies have followed the same methodology.[7]

A number of questions, however, have been raised with reference to the whole enterprise of utilizing modern sociological theories in interpreting the New Testament documents and communities.[8] In the first place, there is the historical distance of nineteen hundred years. This gulf is a problem because the models are concepts developed on the basis of personal observation of contemporary movements and cults. We note for example that Byran Wilson's typological system, which James Wilde uses, was based on a study of Western religious movements.[9] That type of procedure contains two vast discrepancies, the first being temporal and the second being cultural—the attempt being to impose a twentieth-century Western model upon a first-century Eastern culture.[10] Thus it seems that Robin Scroggs is correct when he points out that these sociological theories cannot be awarded the same status of absolute objectivity that one would give to natural laws: "They are rather the time- and culture-bound creatures of humans."[11]

The second problem stems from the strain that many authors seem to evidence when they attempt to force the data from the models to fit their theories. For example, Gerd Theissen attempts to find wandering charismatics even where it seems incredible—he views the Holy Spirit in Matthew 12:32 as representing wandering charismatics.[12]

A third problem that some see as arising from the use of these models is the theological incompatibility with them.

Many Christians accept the New Testament documents as not just religious writings but as works produced under the inspiration of the Holy Spirit. Thus they have a divine and, in many instances, a nonrational element; divine inspiration is most likely not a feature of many modern cults. Daniel Harrington, among others, is of the opinion that the models drawn from sociology of religion and cultural anthropology have no method to deal with this element.[13]

Further, we must ask whether the use of any one model does justice to the facts at hand. To dwell exclusively upon one theory to the exclusion of others certainly will yield a distorted picture of the social reality of the community.

In spite of the above criticisms we are not prepared to throw out the whole enterprise of using sociological models. For these theories provide us with some vital tools that can be used to gain a clearer understanding of the data, and they raise new questions and suggest new answers.[14] We must be aware, however, that theoretical models are only tentative and suggestive. The fact that there is a multiplicity of models demonstrates this. Thus a single theoretical model cannot delineate a true picture of the social realities of any community in the New Testament. The closest we can come to such an assessment is through use of a multiplex approach, that is, an approach which involves eclecticism and pluralism. And even then we may not be near reality.

It seems, however, that the greatest mistake presently being made by New Testament scholars who are utilizing the theoretical approach is the tendency to put "the cart before the horse"—they evaluate a community or a document sociologically without *first* doing a thorough socio-historical description of the community from the data the document itself supplies.[15] This causes some scholars to wonder if after having done a socio-historical description first, there is any need to go then to the model or theory.[16] We must admit that it is possible that sociological theories (based on a description of the social cosmos) will bring an added dimension to the understanding of communities and documents of the New Testament.[17] However, it is the methodological presupposition of the present work that initially an exegetical, socio-historical description is most valuable.

This study does not propose a full-scale sociological description of the community of James; rather it deals only with the theme of poverty and wealth in that community. The procedure is two-fold: (1) The relevant passages are examined exegetically. We discuss those pericopes in which James explicitly refers to the poor and rich and the economic situation of the community—that is, James 1:9–11; 2:1–13; 4:13–5:6. In this initial procedure we look at each of these passages in its literary context and do a grammatical and syntactical analysis of phrases, words, and particles that lead to an understanding of the author's conception of the poor and rich. (2) The concepts of poverty and wealth are examined in their social context, utilizing data and paradigms external to the text (such as physio-geographical, economic, and cultural data of the first century) in an effort to understand the text and its intent. The data, however, are used critically, for we recognize that sources such as Josephus and the Rabbinic literature are problematical and that we must bear in mind the apologetic thrust of the one and the historical framework of the other.

In order to place James's concerns in their wider and more general context, it is necessary that we first briefly discuss the social stratification of the first century A.D. and also look at the general questions of the poor and rich in the biblical literature, as well as in analogous literature and in nonbiblical communities. The first two chapters will briefly deal with these issues.

AUTHORSHIP, DATE, AUDIENCE, AND SETTING OF THE EPISTLE

Although the issues of the authorship, date, audience, and setting of the Epistle of James have been dealt with extensively in commentaries, introductions, and a number of essays, it seems necessary that we set forth our general positions on these matters and make clear the presuppositions on which the arguments of this presentation are built.

The questions of who wrote the document and when it was written are clearly intertwined. There are basically two conjectures: one is the traditional position, which argues for an early date and the authorship by James, Jesus' brother; the other position argues for a late date and pseudonymity.

Donald Guthrie in his *New Testament Introduction* discusses six points of evidence for the traditional view.[18] In the first place, the author identifies himself simply as James, and of the two foremost Jameses in the New Testament James the brother of Jesus played the more prominent part in the life of the early church (James the son of Zebedee having been martyred in A.D. 44). Second, the author reflects a Jewish background. It is true that the epistle has some Hellenistic features, but it is also true that the author reflects a Judeo-Christian milieu steeped in the Old Testament tradition.[19] Third, there are a number of parallels between the Epistle of James and the speech attributed to the James of Acts 15. Even though it is fairly certain that Luke is not giving the very words of James, the similarities are so remarkable that it is difficult to dismiss them as mere accidents of speech. Fourth, in a like vein, James displays very great similarities to Jesus' teaching, particularly in Matthew. The Epistle of James certainly has a relationship with most of the documents of the New Testament, but its relationship with Matthew is most striking and suggests that they grew out of the same tradition.[20] Fifth, and similar to the preceding two points, the Epistle of James is in agreement with the New Testament account of James—which portrayed him, for example, as a transitional figure standing between the full freedom of the gospel and Jewish ritualism. Finally, the social conditions of the community described in the epistle indicate an authorship that predates the destruction of Jerusalem. More will be said on this when we deal with the date and focus on the social description of the rich and poor in the epistle. Suffice it to say that it seems obvious that the author was well acquainted with economic conditions of Jerusalem prior to its fall and depicted them in his epistle. Briefly we must mention also that there are three main objections to the authorship of James the brother of Jesus.[21] First, it is argued that the external evidence for the epistle's not having been accepted in the early church makes contention for the traditional authorship dubious. If the author of the epistle were Jesus' brother, the argument goes, the epistle would have been known much earlier and would have been readily accepted. However, the fact that the epistle was neglected until Origen, who accepted it and used it as scripture is certainly not a conclusive argument one way or the other. Second, some claim that James's attitude to law in the epistle is quite different from that of the James in Acts or Galatians, for the James of Acts and Galatians focuses on the ritual aspect of the law while the epistle emphasizes the moral requirements. However, two points should be made clear here: *(a)* James in Acts and Galatians is not portrayed as a Judaizer; and *(b)* should the epistle be dated before the intense conflict which led to the Jerusalem Council of Acts 15, it is not surprising that the ritual controversy is not mentioned. Besides, the thrust of the epistle is quite different from the other two reports. Third, possibly the strongest objection against the traditional authorship has to do with the language of the epistle. It is claimed that a Palestinian peasant could not write in such a high koine Greek style.[22] This, however, is an a priori argument. There is no reason why James, as well as other Palestinians, could not have been bilingual, speaking Greek—the lingua franca of the empire—as well as their native Aramaic. Furthermore, he could have employed a scribe who wrote in a high style.[23] It is our position, therefore, that the tradition of attributing the epistle to James the brother of Jesus and the head of the early church in Jerusalem is well founded.

As with the question of authorship, there are traditional

and nontraditional positions toward the dating of the epistle—that is to say, the epistle is dated before the death of James, the Lord's brother, in A.D. 62,[24] or between the final decades of the first century and the first part of the second. Scholars divide into three main camps: (1) those who regard the epistle as pseudepigraphous and thus assign it to the nontraditional period;[25] (2) those who place it between A.D. 50 and A.D. 62;[26] and (3) those who date it as prior to A.D. 50.[27] We have already rejected the first position by accepting the authorship of James, the leader of the primitive Jerusalem church.[28] We need only to decide now which of the two latter positions seems the most feasible based on the data in the document.

Essentially there are two arguments used for dating the epistle between A.D. 50 and James's death. The first makes much of the justification passage in James 2:14–26. It is argued that because of the similarities to phrases used by Paul, James must have been attempting to correct a misuse and misunderstanding of the Pauline teaching.[29] This argument, however, is based on a misunderstanding of the theme of faith and works in both authors. The second argument is, we believe, one from silence. It contends that the paucity of distinctive Christian teachings in the epistle is due to the fact that they are presupposed and implies a settled theological condition.[30] Arguments from silence are precarious.

We tend toward the position that the epistle was written before A.D. 50.[31] A basic reason for this position is that the epistle presupposes the social position of the primitive Palestinian community, particularly Jerusalem, prior to the Apostolic Council. Gerhard Kittel may be correct in arguing that "if according to Galatians 2:10 Paul promised to think of the poor in Jerusalem then it is clear that at this time the early Jerusalem community was in a very oppressed situation."[32] It would seem that it is to this situation that James is addressing his diatribe.

The question of the community of the epistle is vital to an

understanding of the document's social setting that we shall describe in this study. At this point we must be aware of the different relationships between a particular document and the community to which it is addressed or out of which it grows.[33] It is possible that some documents do not represent the viewpoints of the community but challenged them,[34] while, on the other hand, they could be descriptions of either the circle of the author himself or of the addressees who live elsewhere. However, it is generally accepted that the Epistle of James represents a true-life situation of a community. Which community this is can be determined only by first understanding who the "twelve tribes of the dispersion" (James 1:1) are.

The view is held widely, particularly by those who postulate a late date for the epistle, that the use of the term *diaspora* here is a way of describing spiritual Israel (i.e., the Christian community).[35] Although many traditionalists refute this interpretation of the term,[36] those who endorse it argue that in reality the Diaspora consisted not only of those driven from their homeland for political reasons, but also of those who were exiled due to their tax debts—the Diaspora was made up of those driven abroad as fugitives, mercenaries, slaves, and penniless persons.[37] Thus the Diaspora is seen as a "worldwide organization of a nation and religion, permeating an immense empire and extending far beyond its frontiers."[38]

If this was the case, then the suggestion is valid that if the author is James of Jerusalem, he is aiming his epistle at a community that his speech cannot reach, that is, one outside Palestine.[39] However, the idea that the Diaspora is outside Palestine may not be correct. F. J. Foakes Jackson and Kirsopp Lake have pointed out that in Palestine the Jews were in many instances truly a dispersion (even though Jackson and Lake do not give any clear and direct evidence that the technical term *diaspora* was used of Palestinian Jews). They write:

In the days of the Maccabees, for example, Galilee had so few Jews that they could be rounded up and settled around Jerusalem by Judas. . . . When Jesus sent His disciples to visit the cities and villages of Galilee, He warned them, "go not into the way of Gentiles, and into the city of the Samaritans enter ye not." This is conclusive proof that in the time of Christ it was necessary for an Israelite travelling in Palestine to discriminate between one of his own towns and those of strangers.[40]

It would seem also that many Jews who were not from Jerusalem were found in the city. The Acts of the Apostles speaks of Parthians, Medes, Elamites, and residents of Mesopotamia, Judea, Cappadocia, Pontus, Asia, Phrygia, Pamphylia, Egypt, Libya, Rome, and so on, as living in Jerusalem (Acts 2:5-11). Besides, many of these diasporic Jews formed separate communities and had their own synagogues, as is evidenced from a synagogue inscription from Jerusalem.[41]

It seems, therefore, to us that James was writing primarily to a community in Palestine—and possibly Syria[42]—with whose background he was familiar and in which he lived.[43] It is certainly true that one senses in those passages that speak of the social situation a very strong personal engagement and passion,[44] which suggests that the author depicts the situation in which he lives and with images that could be drawn only from personal observation.[45] However, we must be careful not to say that James is addressing only Jewish Christians of his community and that he is excluding the non-Christian Jews of the community. This distinction between Christians and non-Christians may very well be artificial. We, therefore, tend to agree with Adolf Schlatter that

> the apostle did not really have in mind two distinct communities side by side, Jewish and Christian going their separate ways. Such a complete separation did eventually come about. . . . But in the Epistle of St. James we still hear a man of the earlier period when the

initial aim of Christianity still held the field, *one* people of God, *one* holy community.[46]

Finally one last word on the unity of the epistle. Due to the influence of Form Criticism, the view has been widely accepted that the Epistle of James is a loosely constructed group of sayings without any cohesion of thought or design.[47] There is, however, a growing challenge to this assumption, and there is now a move in the direction of Redaction Criticism.[48] One of the most recent figures in this enterprise is Peter Davids, who discusses Redaction Criticism's concerns about James in "Themes in the Epistle of James Which Are Judaistic in Character."[49] Davids finds the epistle theologically united—it is primarily *Leidenstheologie;* that is, a theology of suffering is the cental focus of the document. This suggestion is a viable proposition, for it is most evident from James's concern for the poor and oppressed and for social justice that his focus is on a suffering community.[50]

CHAPTER 1

Social Stratification
in the First Century A.D.

The social concern of the Epistle of James, though arising out of the immediate milieu of Palestine, was affected by the wider social matrix of the Greco-Roman world of the first century. It is therefore important that some note be made regarding the general, international social situation that possibly informed James with specific reference to the stratification in society.

Before we enter into this brief overview, three important points must be made. First, it must be noted that the social conditions of the first-century Roman world cannot be viewed as a sudden development. On the contrary, their roots go back into the Hellenistic period.[1] The social and economic atmosphere of the first century has its heritage in Hellenism. Therefore, a brief overview of the Hellenistic impact on the social world is necessary.

Second, we must be careful not to read back into the first century the class structure of today's Western society. Thus, for example, we should not begin with the presupposition that the ancient world had a three-tiered class system: lower, middle, and upper class. We should not blindly insist that there was a middle class in the urban industrial and commercial segments of the population, as it is found in the twentieth century.[2] This point applies to the whole social phenomenon of the ancient world—we must allow the data to speak for themselves.

Third, it is distorting reality to attempt to view the various factors that play a role in the social reality of the first century independent of each other. Economic, ecological, political, cultural, educational, and religious factors are all intertwined, and each is related to the others. However, economics is the single agent that runs through the whole social system and causes all the factors to be closely interrelated. Therefore, much of the discussion below focuses on economics.

Before looking at the role economics played in this particular period of the Roman Empire, we must take cognizance of the economic structures in the Hellenistic Age. It must be observed, however, that evidence about the economic features of the Hellenistic period between Alexander and Augustus is very scanty. Furthermore, the difficulty is intensified because in many cases it is impossible to ascertain whether some features of economic life during the Hellenistic period were not operative in previous centuries. And it is also very difficult to discriminate between the economic life of the Hellenistic period and that of the early Roman Empire.[3]

There seems to be general agreement, however, that the world under the Hellenistic rulers reached a level of capitalistic organization in agriculture, industry, and commercial trading that was not evident prior to the period and that Rome could not surpass. As a matter of fact, it has been suggested that the organization approached in a surprising measure the capitalistic structure of Europe and the United States at the beginning of the twentieth century.[4]

The economic policy of the Greek rulers, particularly the Seleucids, was part of their overall strategy—political, religious, social—to keep their empire united. Thus, for example, export trade played a very important role in the economy of the Greek Empire, not only producing large revenues to the kings and much profit to the Greek and native inhabitants, but also interconnecting various parts of the empire. Trade routes were developed particularly between Syria and Central Asia, and between India and Arabia by land; and among Syria, the Persian Gulf, and Rhodes by sea.[5] The Seleucids also created islands of Greek agriculture in the empire by encouraging wealthy Greek-Macedonians to emigrate and by giving them large tracts of land in the reaches of the empire.[6] This aided in the expansion of the Greek capitalistic system and, in turn, brought great prosperity to the empire.

At the same time, however, the benefits of this widespread increase of prosperity only accrued to the great proprietors and not to common people. As a matter of fact, this economic success was achieved on the heels of intensive economic exploitation, which was a natural consequence of the social unconcernedness of the Hellenistic rulers and their imitators. Thus these capitalists, concentrating exclusively on economics, exacerbated the situation of the lower strata of society. It is interesting to note with Martin Hengel that economic oppression

> prepared the ground for apocalyptic speculation and later revolts, which had increasingly strong social elements, right down to the time of the Bar Kochba rebellion. Even the milieu of the parables of Jesus, with its great landowners, tax farmers, administrators, moneylenders, day labourers and custom officials . . . , can only be understood on the basis of economic conditions brought about by Hellenism in Palestine.[7]

The fact that Hellenism so influenced the Roman Empire and its life makes viable the suggestion that Augustus had no special economic policy; rather the policy of laissez-faire prevailed. He followed a policy of doing what he thought was best for the empire's political and social life. Thus, he refrained from regulating the economic life and accepted the existing conditions with very little modification. These policies of Augustus and the economic conditions of the period continued during the Julio-Claudian era (A.D. 14–70). The difference between this latter period and the Augustan era possibly consisted in the degree of their economic development and some new factors emerging in the Julio-Claudian era.[8]

One important innovation that sets Roman economic achievement apart from the preceding Hellenistic approach is the application of the mechanistic worldview to the everyday problems of the marketplace, thereby producing technological answers. William White, Jr., notes that

> it is impossible to isolate Rome's monetary and economic activities from her technological prowess. Roman success in exploitation of the natural and human resources of the Mediterranean basin was in direct proportion to her efficiency in obtaining, processing, transporting and distributing those natural resources, and the products made from them throughout the Empire.[9]

This conclusion by White does not negate, however, the fact that the Roman emperors followed a policy of laissez-faire economics not only in Italy but throughout the empire's colonies. One need only to look at Egypt and Syro-Palestine for examples.

In Egypt the social and economic life of the natives was based on the conditions of Egyptian religious, social, and economic life from time immemorial. As in previous eras the population was divided into classes, but the peasants who tilled the soil were in the majority, and slavery did not play a significant role in the economic life of Egypt. The state played a leading role in the economic activity of Egypt, with its highly centralized and nationalized economy, all branches of activity being supervised and monopolized by the state. The ruler owned the land, and he let it out to the tillers, who became his lessees. The same policy was used in the case of trade and transportation. With the possible exception of those in Alexandria, all traders and transporters were concessionaries of the state.[10]

With the immigration of Greek and other foreign people a new phenomenon appeared in Egyptian economic life. These new settlers were independent businesspeople who, unlike the natives, did not work for the king and therefore brought with them the idea of private property. This is evident in a statement by Philo regarding a cessation of business in A.D. 38 in Alexandria: "The tradespeople *(Tōn poritōn)* had lost their stocks,[11] and no one, husbandman *(georgous)*,[12] shipman, merchant, artisan, was allowed to practice his usual business."[13]

The new business element was mostly confined to Alexandria, while most of the country remained as it was before—the natives continued in agriculture, in industry, and in transportation as lessees of the state. In this way the economic policy of laissez-faire prevailed in Egypt under Roman rule.

Of more interest to us—especially in light of material to be discussed below—is Syro-Palestine. At the outset it should be made clear that the areas of the empire between Asia Minor and Egypt were interdependent economically and had close cultural connections. The fact that the region was viewed as one is attested to by the ancient geographer Strabo, who views Judea as part of Syria. According to him, Syria is bound on the north by Cilicia, Mount Amanus, and the Euphrates, and on the south by Arabia and Egypt.[14] Even the Jewish rabbis recognized this close connection, for Akiba laid down the general rule: "The like of whatsoever is permitted to be done in the Land of Israel may be done also in Syria."[15] It, therefore, seems valid for us to discuss as a unit the economic situation of Syria and Palestine because so much is similarly characteristic of the whole region.[16]

Roman domination over the Syrian region was only a brief

episode in the life of the territory. Therefore, Rome did not have the time necessary to transform the country radically. However, it has been demonstrated that the economic conditions in Syro-Palestine improved under Augustus and his successors. Many new cities and towns were built, and the weight of Roman technology was brought to bear on the economic growth.[17] There may be truth, therefore, in the suggestion that "the *Pax Romana* of the Age of Augustus had positive consequences for Palestine in terms of trade and commerce" as well as in terms of other socioeconomic factors.[18]

The *Pax Romana* also had negative consequences. True, because of it new groups found their way into the upper class—for example, the family of Herod—and thus benefited greatly from economic growth. However, the economic situation of the ordinary people became increasingly worse. Besides, the same Roman technology that was used to improve the economic situation was used for economic exploitation and aggravated the accompanying poverty.[19] The few examples of great fortunes in Syro-Palestine should not blind us to the widespread poverty among the masses of people. How pathetic this was is demonstrated in Rabbi Ishmael's reaction when he wept and said, "The daughters of Israel are comely but poverty destroys their comeliness."[20] It was an intolerable situation in which impoverishment and chronic insecurity were the lot of the members of the lower class, these conditions being brought on by a small group of financiers who dispossessed and oppressed them.

It is clear that even though the economic situation was improving under Roman domination, this improvement benefited only a very small segment of the population. The vast majority of the peoples of the empire lived in appalling poverty. Thus it becomes more and more evident that it was not merely political dissatisfaction or religious fanaticism that brought unrest throughout the empire. The root cause of the misery was economic.

Although we began with the fact that economics under-girded the various social factors at work in the Roman Empire, religion also played a vital role in the delineation of the social stratification of the empire. Thus it seems necessary that we deal with it apart from the economic question.

Class status and affiliation were important factors in determining one's religious beliefs, activities, and associations. John G. Gager, in his essay "Religion and Social Class in the Early Roman Empire," deals with the various classes and orders in the empire and shows their characteristic religious leanings and tendencies. In the first place, the basic instinct of the senatorial class was conservative. Its members looked to the ancient gods and cults that had established and that continued to support their privileged position. However, Gager points out that "these ancient cults, like the more recent imperial cult, were primarily socio-political in character, with little evidence that their adherents regarded them as anything but routine civic institutions."[21]

Below the senators in social as well as legal status were the equestrians or knights. These were the capitalists in business, commerce, and industry. Their administrative ability made them invaluable assets in the administration of the empire. An example of their power and control is found in Palestine where the province of Judea was administered by equestrians from A.D. 6–41 and also from A.D. 44–66. With regard to their religious adherence—although the information is scanty—it seems obvious that they, like the senators, would adhere to the ancient gods and imperial cults that supported the status quo.

As we move to the various municipal bureaucracies of the empire, we find Rome's policy of maintaining good relations with its conquered people displayed in its attitude to the religion and customs of these people. Thus, for example, Jewish residents in cities throughout the empire and particularly in Jerusalem were allowed to elect their own bureaucrats and follow their ancient religious practices. Palestine was a classic example of how religious life and socioeconomic and political factors were closely bound together.[22] In Palestine the aristocratic Sadducees dominated the Sanhedrin (especially during the Herodian dynastic rule) and remained loyal to Rome.[23] These men were not only leaders in society and religion, but also were capitalists and merchants on a large scale who obtained much of their wealth through speculation, lodging it in the national bank, that is, the Jerusalem Temple.[24]

The religious adherence of the lower classes in the empire—plebeians, freedmen, slaves, for example—varied. In the main, however, they were devotees to cults such as those that worshiped Cybele, Mithras, Dionysius, Isis, Serapis, and so on. Furthermore, the supernatural and belief in astrology and chance all played a great part in the life of these people.[25] To these forces they turned for satisfaction and authority, for the ancient gods and cults brought satisfaction only to those in the upper classes.

The best example of the lower classes' attempt to find satisfaction in a new religion is that of primitive Christianity's appeal almost exclusively to them. It was not until the second century that the well-to-do upper class began to join the church in any great number and, as Ernst Troeltsch notes, "This change did not take place without a good deal of opposition on the part of the educated and wealthy sections of Society."[26] The fact of primitive Christianity's appeal primarily to those in the lower classes demonstrates that the religion of the early Christians and the existing social situation were closely intertwined. Furthermore, the growth of Christianity is only one manifestation of the way in which social, political, religious, and economic forces interacted in Roman society.

In the sphere of education, stratification was not so much between learned and unlearned as between the rich and poor. Economics was at the root of all social divisions. One needs only to note Louis Finkelstein's discussion regarding the tension between the scholar and the *'am ha-'aretz* to see the difference in the educational levels of the rich and the poor.[27]

There is no doubt about it—there was a high level of educational output in the empire:

> Mechanical knowledge was by no means wanting and numerous useful inventions were known. A high degree of efficiency was displayed in the acquisition of food, clothing, and shelter. Agriculture, industry, trade, and commerce were carried on in such a fashion as to meet, in a comparatively adequate way, the needs of the time. The science of legislation and government had received careful attention, and had been developed to a stage where they furnished effective protection for society. Nor had the recreational side of life been ignored. The theatre, the amphitheatre, the circus, the stadium, all afforded ample opportunity for entertainment and diversion. Cultural interests had also found satisfaction in the cultivation of literature, painting, architecture, and sculpture.[28]

But all these educational and cultural opportunities were limited only to the upper strata of society.[29] There are abundant contemptuous references by this class to the lack of education of the lower class—particularly the rural class. For example, it was said that "country folk had read no books, [and] their choice of words was out of date and uncouth."[30]

In light of the low economic status of most early Christians, it seems quite probable that the educational level of the members of the church was also quite low. In contrast to later Gnostics, most early Christians were nonintellectuals. It has been suggested, however, that the lowest educational level that should be reasonably assumed for the New Testament writers is the equivalent of the upper level of secondary-school instruction.[31] Yet the educational level of the writers is not a true indicator of the educational level of the adherents; rather a social description of each community to which a document was addressed is the best way to arrive at a true assessment of the adherents' level of education.

As a final note, it is imperative in looking at the social structure of the Roman Empire that one take cognizance of the urban-rural relations and conflicts. This was a very important factor in the economic, cultural, and religious life of the empire and in Christianity. The distinction between rural and urban was less in some parts of the empire, such as Asia Minor, Macedonia, and Greece. But we find with the growing urbanization of these areas that rural people began flocking to the cities and thus bringing urban-rural tensions and conflicts there. It was because of this that the earliest Pauline Christianity was an urban phenomenon.[32]

A classic example of the urban-rural relations is to be found in Palestine. While the urban population was rising throughout most of the Mediterranean basin, the bulk of the population in Palestine was still rural, and its agricultural life stood boldly against the growing urbanization.[33] Thus it is true that early Palestinian Christianity was rural in character and, like other renewal movements of the time, had its root in the hinterland and was hostile to Jerusalem.[34]

The problem of the conflictual relationship between town and country in Palestine actually goes back to the beginning of the Second Commonwealth. The increased importance accorded Jerusalem during this period made the opposition between it and the rural areas very sharp. The sophisticated urban patricians of the city—with their bureaucratic, hierarchial connections and superior wealth—regarded those who followed the team and plough with pitying condescension.[35]

The distinction between the urban and rural populations, however, became more pronounced in the first century, and with it followed increased antagonism. The countryside was restless, mainly because of the exploitation of the urban capitalists. The average rural person had become a client of an absentee landlord who lived in the city. This was one cause of the peasants' hatred of the city. The city was perceived to represent a specially privileged class from which the peasant felt systematically excluded.[36]

Rural-urban relations in Judea finally broke down into actual warfare. One can hardly doubt that it was the rural elements that formed the most dynamic factor in the war against Rome. The Zealot party, which was representative of the Palestinian, mainly Judean, peasant piety, showed hostility toward the rich of the city, the upper priesthood of the Temple, and the foreign rulers; and the Zealots led the drive toward social change.[37] In their overall strategy of achieving a more just order in society, they took up arms against the establishment in the first part of the first century. The Jewish War amply illustrates the tensions in the social structure in the Roman Empire during that century.

CHAPTER 2

Poor and Rich in Jewish
and Christian Literature

The context of the Epistle of James is not only the Greco-Roman world of the first century, but also, and most important, the Judeo-Christian worldview. It is, therefore, important that we examine that worldview by taking a cross-sectional look at the problem of poverty and wealth prior to James as well as contemporaneous with him. We will first assess the various traditions about the poor and rich at different epochs of Israelite history—namely, the premonarchial, the monarchial—and in such literature as the sapiential writings and the Psalms. In the postexilic and intertestamental period we will take as our point of departure the apocryphal literature, looking at how each genre—wisdom and apocalyptic, for example—views the concept of poverty and wealth. Following this there will be a description and discussion of first-century (Palestinian and Diasporan) Judaism's attitude toward the poor and rich. We will find it necessary at that point to deal with sectarian Judaism (for example, the Qumran society) separately, because some scholars have used the Qumran model as a paradigm for interpreting James. Finally, we will look at the New Testament material, particularly the Synoptics, Acts, and the Pauline literature. Although we do not believe any of the latter directly influenced James, there is a strong possibility that the traditions behind each could have influenced the epistle.

Throughout all this discussion the question as to the meaning of the concept "poor" is addressed—is it an economic description or a spiritual designation or perhaps both? An answer to this question is crucial if we are accurately to interpret James. It is upon the conclusion drawn to that question that a social study of the type being undertaken in this book stands or falls.

THE OLD TESTAMENT LITERATURE

The various Old Testament traditions about poverty are complex, as is the terminology describing the state.[1] A brief survey of the key words that are usually translated as "poor" will illustrate this.[2] The Hebrew term *'ani* refers to a person who is dependent in an economic sense—to one who is humiliated, dispossessed, and in a state of lowliness and distress. *'Ani,* like its root *'anah* and *'anaw,* thus depicts the poor, needy, oppressed, and afflicted. However, the word can also be translated as "humble" and "meek," thereby leading some to see a more religious nuance in it.[3] A poor person is also designated by *dal* and *'ebyon.* The former indicates one who is socially weak, frail, and helpless, while the latter denotes one who begs alms, one who lacks and awaits something from another. The favorite word in the wisdom literature for "poor" is *rush,* which refers to the person who is poor, needy, and famished.

PREMONARCHIAL PERIOD

In premonarchial Israel the distinction between the poor and rich seemed to be unknown. Instead a "clan egalitarianism" existed.[4] The close tribal and family units ensured that no one starved—each one in the clan and family had equal rights and status.[5] The books of Exodus, Leviticus, and Deuteronomy, however, deal with the question of the poor and the land. The ideal state of affairs that Yahweh intended for his covenanted people is that there should be no poverty among them. Thus it is declared:

> There will be no poor among you (for the Lord will bless you in the land which the Lord your God gives you for an inheritance to possess), if only you will obey the voice of the Lord your God, being careful to do all this commandment which I command you this day [Deut. 15:4,5].

But because Israel was a rebellious, covenant-violating people, and because undercurrents of social and economic problems were beginning to undermine the sedentary society of the Israelites in Canaan and to create greater distinctions and tensions among the classes,[6] Israel elicited the words, "the poor will never cease out of the land" (Deut. 15:11). However, this was not an excuse for ignoring the needy. On the contrary, they were to receive special consideration, and stipulations were made to that effect (Deut. 15:7–11).

MONARCHIAL PERIOD

The social problems of sedentary life in Israel were accentuated—particularly in the period of the monarchy—with increased trade and commerce, the development of an urban society in the royal cities of Jerusalem and Samaria (and thus the rural-urban tensions), and widening class distinction. A large majority of the population fell in the category of the poor and deprived, while there was a small stratum of plutocratic and aristocratic landowners. It was this rich upper stratum of society that destroyed the clan egalitarianism and rejected Yahweh's covenant ideal for the Israelites. It was against this class that the classical prophets raised their voices of denunciation.

These prophets took up the cause of the poor and proclaimed that one of Israel's chief sins was the oppression and exploitation of the poor due to the merciless desire of some to increase their wealth. The prophets saw a very close relationship between this situation and the moral breakdown in society.[7] Julian Morgenstern succinctly summarizes the lot of this exploited class:

> In such a society the poor had little chance. Involved in litigation with wealthy and powerful neighbours, witnesses were turned against them by one consideration or another. Perjured testimony was offered and was readily accepted by judges as corrupt and self-seeking as those who bribed them. Pledges were taken for the payment of debts, and even when the latter were duly paid, the pledges were not returned. Very many, unable otherwise to pay their debts, would be sold no doubt by court order, or else would sell a son or perhaps a daughter, or even their very own selves, as slaves in the hope that thereby enough might be realized to discharge the debt.[8]

It is in this context that Yahweh consistently calls for justice to be done to alleviate the social condition of the poor. And it is also within this context that we must understand the admonition of Micah 6:8: "He has showed you, O man, what is good; and what does the Lord require of you, but to do justice and to love kindness, and to walk humbly with your God."[9]

WISDOM LITERATURE

Unlike most of the rest of the Old Testament, the wisdom writings are very positive regarding wealth. The sages viewed poverty as being self-incurred—a thought that was foreign to the prophetic writings.[10] The poor are poor because they seek after pleasure and are frivolous, because they ignore instruction and reproof, and because they are too hasty.[11]

On the other hand, the rich are praised. Their wealth is viewed as a sign of God's blessing, and they are constantly placed in a positive light vis-à-vis the poor.[12] Yet there are passages that demonstrate that wealth is viewed positively *only* if the rich one is in a close relation with God.[13] There is also condemnation of the obsession with wealth and of all that which is obtained by devious means.[14] Furthermore, the sages demand justice for the poor and disinherited, and condemn oppression of them.[15]

THE PSALMS

In this literature Yahweh is depicted as one who brings salvation to the poor in affliction, who provides for the needy, who lifts them up from their low situation and makes them sit with princes.[16] Yahweh is also extolled as one who defends and protects the poor and oppressed from their enemies.[17]

The enemies of the poor in the Psalms, however, are not usually called the rich, but the *rash'im*—the wicked. This seems to be a religious term. But in many instances the *rash'im* are also an oppressive social class: they are greedy for gain, have abundance, and afflict the widows, the fatherless, and the poor.[18] As the terms "saint" and "righteous" stand in parallelism, so "wicked" and "rich" are equated. It is the poor who are a type pleasing to Yahweh because of their dependence upon Yahweh for existence and protection. In this way the poor are the humble and pious ones. But they are still the ones who are actually in economic distress.[19]

THE INTERTESTAMENTAL LITERATURE

The postexilic period was one of austerity for the poor. It saw the enrichment of the haves and an aggravation of the increasingly desperate condition of the have nots. In the apocryphal and pseudepigraphical literature we find in a number of places complaints, castigations, and denunciations of the rich and of economic injustice. In the apocalyptic writings the threat of judgment against the rich is very sharp. 1 Enoch 94:8–97:10 is typical:

> Woe to you, ye rich, for ye have trusted in your riches,
> and from your riches shall ye depart. . . .
> Ye have committed blasphemy and unrighteousness
> and have become ready for the day of slaughter. . . .
> Woe unto you, ye sinners, for your riches make you appear like the righteous,
> but your hearts convict you of being sinners. . . .
> Woe to you who devour the finest of the wheat,
> and drink wine in large bowls,
> and tread under foot the lowly with your might. . . .
> Woe to you who acquire silver and gold in unrighteousness and say:
> "We have become rich with riches and possessions . . .
> and our granaries are (brim) full as with water. . . .
> Your riches shall not abide
> but speedily ascend from you.

Here, as in the Psalms, there are religious judgments—the rich, for instance, are equated with unrighteousness; however, the primary reference is to an economic situation.

Also, in the apocalyptic literature is the theme of the Great Reversal: the rich oppressors and exploiters will die in their prosperity and wealth, receive the judgment that was not executed in their lifetimes, and experience eternal damnation, while the faithful and righteous poor will in the life to come receive eternal rewards.[20] We should note, however, that in some of this literature there is present a sense of compassion, generosity, and justice, which suggests that the apocalyptic writers were concerned not only with the spiritual dimension of the future life, but also with the social reality of the present.[21]

The wisdom tradition of the Old Testament is carried on in the sapiential writings of the intertestamental period. Thus, while on the one hand there is a high estimate of wealth and praise for the rich, with accompanying harsh words for the poor,[22] on the other hand there is a polemic uttered against the exploitation, unscrupulous speculation, deceit, and greed of the rich, and there is praise for the poor person's wisdom.[23]

FIRST-CENTURY JEWISH LIFE

PALESTINIAN

From Maccabean times Palestinian Judaism was plagued with severe social tension. This was accentuated under the reign of Herod, whose policies brought great economic pressures on the poor. These policies not only caused the masses to live in dismal poverty, but made more pronounced as well the class distinctions during that period.[24] Illustrative of the distinction are the Sadducees and some Rabbinic teaching on the one hand, and the *'am ha-' aretz* on the other.

The rich agriculturalists, commercial farmers, merchants, and large landowners rallied around the Sadducean hierarchy, and those wealthy persons used the Sadducean theology to justify their attitude to wealth: the Sadducees regarded riches as an expression and constituent part of salvation. Backed by that theology, the wealthy used oppressive means both to obtain their wealth and to keep it.[25]

In the Rabbinic writings we find in a number of instances a high estimate placed on wealth and a commensurate deprecation of poverty. In our discussion of the poor and rich in James we shall deal in more detail with the attitude of the Rabbis. Suffice it to say here that their attitude toward poverty and wealth did not in the least help the lot of the poor.

Over against the Rabbinic and Sadducean classes stood the *'am ha-' aretz*. They were the common, uneducated people. The Rabbinic literature demonstrates that the contempt in which the rich and poor held one another was deep-seated, to the level of deep hatred.[26]

DIASPORAN

The Jews of the dispersion were caught up in the vicious economic differentiation of the first-century Roman Empire—an age that Seneca lamented as bringing to an end the happy age of primitive communism *(consortis)* and in which, he wrote, "avarice and luxury [have] broken the bonds which held mortals together."[27] We have noticed that the poor in Palestine suffered greatly in the first century, but Salo Baron has suggested that economic differentiation in Palestine "was far surpassed by that of the Jewish communities in the dispersion."[28] He further demonstrates this by remarking:

If Palestine, politically autonomous and dependent on local natural and historic factors, was irresistibly drawn into the vortex of Graeco-Roman economic developments, the Jewish minorities in the Diaspora were almost entirely the objects of economic forces beyond their collective control. Particularly those large segments of Jewry forcibly brought to other lands as prisoners of war and slaves had no choice but to adjust themselves to the requirements of their masters.[29]

SECTARIAN

The question of whether the concept of the poor should be understood socioeconomically or pietistically is classically illustrated in the sectarian movement of the Essenes and in the Dead Sea Scrolls. Although it seems the concept was used in some pietistic sense, there is much contextual evidence to indicate that riches, possessions, and poverty were meant to be understood literally. Josephus, for example, writes of the Essenes:

Riches they despise, and their community of goods is truly admirable; you will not find one among them distinguished by greater opulence than another. They have a law that new members on admission to the sect shall confiscate their property to the order, with the result that you will nowhere see either abject poverty or inordinate wealth; the individual's possessions join the common stock and all, like brothers, enjoy a single patrimony.[30]

This attitude is confirmed in the *Manual of Discipline* and *Damascus Document* (or *Zadokite Document)*.[31] Thus as in the Psalms and in some intertestamental literature poverty is basically used as a socioeconomic designation.[32]

THE NEW TESTAMENT LITERATURE

THE SYNOPTICS

Of the two Gospels—Matthew and Luke—on which we will focus our attention, Luke shows more concern regarding the issue of the poor and rich.[33] Robert Karris is correct when he suggests that "the theme of poor and rich holds *a* key to the rich storehouse of Luke-Acts."[34] Throughout Luke's Gospel there is special concern and regard for the poor on the one hand and damnation for the rich and their wealth on the other.

There are many who argue that the concepts of the poor and rich are used in the Gospel of Luke metaphorically, symbolically, and as a technical designation for the Christian community.[35] But even if a case can be made for some symbolic interpretation, there seems to be no question that Luke is addressing mainly real economic conditions.[36] The poor are those who lack the necessities and are oppressed, while the rich are those who have considerable possessions and wealth.[37]

The question arises as to how we shall understand the "poor

in spirit" of the Matthean beatitude vis-à-vis Luke's formulations about the poor in his version of the Beatitudes. It is the current opinion among scholars that the Lukan version emphasizes the social note of Jesus' message, while Matthew stresses the spiritual side and must therefore be interpreted in a purely religious way.[38] However, a comparison of Matthew 5:3–5 with the *Thanksgiving Scroll* of Qumran brings into question that assumption.[39]

D. Flusser, in his article on the problem, notes that all the biblical and exegetical material found in the first three beatitudes of Matthew is paralleled in the sectarian literature, particularly in the *Thanksgiving Scroll.* Of particular interest is the fact that both the scroll and Matthew use the designation "poor in spirit." Commenting upon this, Flusser states that "it is difficult to escape the conclusion that there is an historical connection between the words of Jesus and ideology of the Dead Sea Sect."[40] There is, therefore, a possible connection between the Matthean beatitude and the social framework of the Qumran community (though we will admit that it is possibly true, as Davies notes, that the phrase was a common part of the Semitic milieu).[41]

Flusser is correct when he notes that appelations such as "poor," "pauper," and "needy" "are characterized by a paradoxical combination of a term depicting the abject state of the sect in the present, with a second one which proclaims triumphantly the plenty of God's grace bestowed on His elect."[42] Matthew's beatitude can be understood in the same way. The Evangelist contrasts the present plight of the poor and oppressed with the future glory of the kingdom. But this regard is not for any and every pauper, but only for those who are in the *spiritual realm* of the community. Possibly Flusser is more precise when he suggests that Matthew is referring to those who are "endowed with the supreme gift of divine bliss, with the Holy Spirit."[43] Matthew therefore is not merely spiritualizing an earlier saying that lacked a moralizing element. For Matthew economic poverty was a glaring reality, and he, though with less vehemence than Luke, played upon the motif of the Great Reversal. Even the Great Judgment scene of the Last Discourse (Matt. 25:31-36) describes the physical and economic plight of the oppressed. We agree with Leander Keck, then, that this pericope points back to the Beatitudes[44] and thus forms an inclusion with Matthew 5:3-12 for the discourse material in Matthew's Gospel.

It is in Luke, however, that one finds much more concern over the topic of poverty and wealth. The theme of the Great Reversal—when the coming kingdom will bring help and salvation to the poor and exclude the rich[45]—pervades the Gospel of Luke. From the opening chapters of the Gospel, Luke shows definite sympathies for the poor and oppressed: in the Magnificat, Mary rejoices that God has exalted the lowly and hungry while sending the rich away empty (1:52-53). Opening his ministry at Nazareth, Jesus announces that his mission is to preach good news to the poor (4:18-19), and then later sends a message to John the Baptist that the poor are having the good news preached to them (7:22-23).[46]

On the other hand, Luke presents Jesus as having a negative attitude to riches and the rich. The parable of the rich man who is condemned for accumulating more than he needs while not being rich toward God (12:15-21) is followed by the instruction of Jesus to his disciples to "sell your possessions," for "where your treasure is there will your heart be also" (12:32-34). There are other passages in which Luke describes Jesus as commending those who give up their possessions (e.g., 18:26-30; 19:8-10). Jesus was therefore being consistent when he told the rich young ruler to sell all he had and distribute it to the poor (18:18-23). We must read this narrative literally, just as we must rigorously and literally read Jesus' reply to the ruler in vv. 24-25: "How hard it is for those who have riches to enter the kingdom of God! For it is easier for a camel to go through the eye of a needle than for a rich man to enter the kingdom of God." Robert Grant has noted that the latter part of this saying "was spoiled by later Christians, ever eager to conciliate the rich, who pretended that there was a 'camel gate' at Jerusalem through which a camel could pass only on its knees (!) or, to little effect, invented the meaning 'rope' for the Greek word 'camel'."[47] Later Christians, in other words, attempted to discount or avoid Luke's clear portrayal of Jesus as one who had great concern for the poor and oppressed while being vehemently condemnatory of the rich and their riches.

THE ACTS OF THE APOSTLES

It is generally accepted that Acts is the second part of a complete work by Luke. Therefore one has to understand any concept of poverty and riches in the latter part of the work in light of the first part.

Interestingly, the word *ptōchos* ("poor") does not occur in Acts. However, two passages in the book demonstrate that the primitive church took Jesus' teaching regarding possessions seriously: in both Acts 2:44–47 and 4:32–37 we find that those who had joined the community "sold their possessions and goods and distributed them to all" (2:45).[48] Thus, "there was not a needy person among them for as many as were possessors of land and houses sold them, and brought the proceeds of what was sold" (4:34). This egalitarianism in communal life was thus a feature of the primitive communism of the church. And it is possible that this was in part the motive for many priests (not high priests, who belonged to the wealthy class)[49] becoming members of the community; for, as we shall see later, the economic status of the majority of the priests was dismal.

THE PAULINE LITERATURE

Questions about poverty and wealth were also raised in the Pauline communities. The issue, however, was in a sense different from that in the Palestinian communities. In Paul many of the judgments and actions described in the Synoptics and Acts of the Apostles are left aside. There is no blessing for the poor; there is no condemnation of the rich and their wealth; there is no communal sharing of goods as was practiced in the Jerusalem community.[50] Yet Paul refers to "deep poverty" (2 Cor. 8:2) in the Macedonian church—in the only instance in which he mentions explicitly the economic situation of a group in the Greek world.[51] But the problem of the rich and poor surfaces in the inner social stratification of the Pauline churches, particularly that of Corinth.

Gerd Theissen has shown how the social tension in the Corinthian church was brought about by this stratification.[52] His argument is based on 1 Corinthians 1:26–29. This passage shows that the majority of Pauline converts were from the lower stratum of society. However, it is also implied that there was a minority from the upper social stratum—a dominating minority.[53] When Paul discusses the question of eating meat offered to idols (chaps. 8, 10) and when he attacks the recurring tensions at the Lord's Supper (11:17–34), he is in part addressing the clashes between those two social strata—the "weak" (that is, the poor lower class) and the "strong" (that is, the wealthy upper class).

Theissen's arguments may be tentative and may not be totally accurate in details. However, his essays do enlighten us about the problem of poverty and wealth in the Corinthian community and about Paul's attempt to deal with it. Paul's ideal for the Corinthian church was egalitarianism in all its social life, and he worked toward an egalitarianism both between rich and poor and between male and female.[54]

It has been noted thus far that in its bias against the rich and partiality toward the poor, the early Palestinian Jesus movement (to use Theissen's terminology) was following in the footsteps of the classical Old Testament prophets and of sectarian Judaism. However, as Christianity moved out of its incipiency in the Palestinian milieu and into the Gentile world—where a minority privileged class began dominating the Christian community—the church had to modify its harsh position against the rich and riches but at the same time promote and aim for egalitarianism among its members.[55]

There may be a further reason for this shift in the church's focus: namely, the delay of the Parousia. The very early Christians—like the members of the other apocalyptic movements of that era—saw wealth as holding one captive in the age; they believed that with the arrival of the imminent new age, their position would be reversed. With the delay of the Parousia, the church had to deal with the reality of the social and economic structure of the overall societies in which it found itself and with the relationship between those societies and the individual Christian communities. Those considerations made heavy demands upon the church, and Robert Grant may be right when he states that "as the eschatological enthusiasm waned the philosophical ethic that replaced it reinforced a conservative outlook."[56]

CHAPTER 3

The Great Reversal: James 1:9–11

The motif of the reversal of status, which is evident in the apocalyptic literature of the intertestamental period and also in Luke's Gospel (for example, in the Magnificat and the Beatitudes), comes to the fore at the outset in the Epistle of James. The rich oppressors and exploiters will pass away ignominiously and suddenly with all their prosperity and wealth, while the poor will be exalted.

That the question of the poor person's situation is high on the agenda of James is evident in the fact that it appears so early in the document. How one gauges the intensity of James's interest in this question is affected by how one views the relationship between James 1:9–11 and the preceding verses. There are three positions: (1) there is no connection; (2) the connection goes back to v. 2; and (3) vv. 9–11 are part of the total context of vv. 2–8.

Form critics like Martin Dibelius argue that a new subject is being introduced in vv. 9–11 with no connection with the preceding verses. The passage introduces a new antithesis that has no connection in thought with the antithesis—faith and doubt—in the preceding verses. Therefore the "doubter" (vv. 6–8) should not be identified with either *ho plousios* ("the rich") of v. 10 or *ho tapeinos* ("the poor") of v. 9. For those who hold to this position there is no logical significance to the introductory particle *de* ("but") in v. 9.[1] Dibelius notes, however, that if there is some significance to the *de,* "one would have to suppose a connection which went all the way back to 1:2–4 equating the lowly man with the person proved by means of trials." He feels that this is not intended by the author.[2]

There are others who, although finding no direct connection between vv. 9–11 and vv. 5–8, do believe that the *de* is significant, and they find its point of contact in vv. 2–4. The *de,* therefore, returns to the point of view in vv. 2–4 and picks up the theme of *peirasmoi.* It is these "trials" that fall upon the *tapeinos* of v. 9, but according to James Hardy Ropes they are "not an evil for him but an elevation."[3]

A third group of expositors sees a more total connection between vv. 9–11 and vv. 2–8. F. J. Hort, for example, argues that in vv. 9–11 the author is actually returning to the original theme of v. 2, "bringing in the characteristic contrast of rich and poor as a special application of the principle of rejoicing in trials."[4] However, Hort does view the author as intending to set the unstable one *(akatastatos)* of v. 8 in direct opposition to the poor and rich of vv. 9–11.[5] This third group of expositors seems closest to understanding the intent of James. James is using the introductory *de* purposely to set up an antithesis not only with the *ho plousios* and all that is said about that one or class in vv. 10–11, but also with *anēr dipsiuchos akatastos* ("the double-minded, unstable person") of v.8. Therefore, there does seem to be a parallelism between v. 8 and vv. 10–11. At the same time, v. 9 harks back to vv. 2–4 and can be seen as being in parallelism with those verses: *ho tapeinos* refers to the one meeting various trials, but that one's steadfastness is his or her exaltation.

This parallelism continues in v. 12, where the person who endures trials is the same one who is referred to in v. 2 as well as in v. 9. A beatitude is pronounced on that person. To that person the crown of life is promised. The Great Reversal of fortunes takes place.

In the pericope of vv. 9–11, the author sets up the antithetical parallelism: *ho tapeinos//ho plousios.* The latter term designates "the rich." The primary meaning of the former term is "low" and "flat," and it thus came to mean "lowly," "mean," "insignificant," "weak," and "poor."[6] The term as used in the LXX corresponds to the Hebrew terms *'ani* and *dal,* which represent the poor, oppressed, and afflicted one.[7] There seems to be no question that James is dealing with the antithesis of the poor and rich in these verses.

We earlier discussed the possibility that the concept of "the poor" has both a physical as well as a spiritual connotation. Likewise it is argued that *tapeinos* can refer to both an outward condition of poverty and oppression and an inner spiritual condition with reference to one's character.[8] The question here is to which of these is the author alluding.

It is hard for some to adjudicate whether the poor in James are economically poor or whether they belong to the so-called *anawin*-piety (i.e., those who are devout and pious before God) of Judaism, that group that referred to themselves as "The Poor."[9] Others hold that the term is not economic, but is purely religious.[10] They argue that in v. 9 the term is used metaphorically and poetically to describe the pious or the Christian. Thus James and his community remain in the theological world of the "pious poor."[11]

Still other commentators contend that James's thought must not be spiritualized. They set aside all explanations which make *ho tapeinos* mean the Christian who is "lowly in spirit." They state that the "lowly one" here is envisaged as the poor one in the social sense—one who is oppressed by poverty brought on by the unscrupulous rich.[12]

An absolute either/or position here, however, seems to be a faulty option. To separate the economically poor and oppressed from the pious in James's community seems to be wrong. And, as Meinrad Stenzel points out, it may be that in vv. 9–11 "we are encountering the after effects of the late Old Testament idea that only those who are bereft of possessions can truly be devoted to God."[13] At the same time, James's characterization of the poor vis-à-vis the rich throughout his epistle amply demonstrates that his emphasis is on the social station of those classes.[14]

Verses 10–11 focus on the second part of the antithesis and, throughout the rest of the document, it is this aspect that James dwells on at length. It is the downfall of the rich that he emphasizes. As we approach v. 10 we encounter what seems to be a major difficulty, namely, what we shall supply before and after *ho plousious*. It is generally agreed that *kauchasthō* ("let him boast") should be understood at the opening of the verse, but there is no such agreement on whether or not *adelphos* ("brother") is also to be understood as referring to *ho plousious*. Because v. 9 forms an antithetical parallelism with v. 10, it would seem at first glance that both *kauchasthō* and *adelphos* would be required to complete the parallelism.[15] But the solution is not as simple as that, for there seems to be no trace of brotherly relationship in the harsh words of vv. 10–11.[16]

Actually, the two positions on the question of whether to supply "brother" or not are based on how explicators answer the question of whether "the rich" James refers to is a Christian or a non-Christian. We might ask whether the author is speaking heroically or ironically in regards to the downfall of the rich. Those who hold to the heroic interpretation usually argue that James is speaking to rich Christians; those who believe that James is speaking ironically contend that he is addressing rich non-Christians.

The argument set forth by Ropes is the one usually followed by those who hold that James is speaking heroically. Ropes suggests that it is more natural to supply the word "brother." Besides, the *tapeinōsei* ("humiliation") refers to the outward humiliation and loss of goods which is brought on by the "trials" referred to in v. 2. Thus the rich are enjoined to display a heroism in face of the loss of earthly possessions, presumably for something better.[17] Of course with this interpretation both *tōi hupsei* ("exaltation") and *tapeinōsei* would refer to the same experiences. However, according to Ropes, even though the terms refer to similar experiences they are "not quite parallel expressions, since *hupsos* is used of a *moral and spiritual* exaltation, *tapeinōis* of external and material humiliation."[18] Yet if humiliation has some parallel with exaltation, it would be in the sense of "humility," says Burton Scott Easton, and that according to him would be reading too much into the word.[19] It is, therefore, wise to read the words as they stand and not to seek to interpret them by reading into them something that is not there, especially since as a rule the author is far from being ambiguous in his language.[20]

Ropes admits only two chief objections to this position: first, elsewhere in the document when the rich are spoken of the reference is to wicked persons outside the Christian community; second, *papeleustai* of v. 10 has to denote the loss of wealth, and v.11 also should be understood in a corresponding sense.[21] How this last point is a problem to Ropes's argument is not clear, nor does he attempt a rebuttal to either of the objections. One of the main difficulties with this point of view is the fact that it is the *rich person,* not merely the riches, who passes away; and so it is also in v. 11.[22]

Those who press for the ironic interpretation contend that "brother" should not be inserted, and they thus believe the author is not necessarily speaking to a Christian. According to this position the author is serious regarding the boasting of the poor in v. 9, but he is speaking ironically in the case of the rich in vv. 10–11: "The rich man has had his day; all he can expect from the future is humiliation; that is the only thing left for him to 'boast about.' This would then be some 'boast'!"[23] In other words, the rich man has had his day of success; all the future holds for him is disaster; let him boast in that if he can!

For Ropes this interpretation involves serious difficulties. He lists three: (1) the refusal to supply "brother" is unnatural; (2) the irony that is suggested in the understood "let him boast" is excessive; and (3) "the lack of adaptation of the thought in any way to the idea of *peirasmoi* . . . still seems to govern the context."[24] The first two objections are very subjective. With regards to the last, what Ropes fails to realize is the fact that while *peirasmoi* governs the context, this does not mean that it governs every detail of the passage. Thus the concept can govern the first part of the antithesis; the other part is only an illustration of the contrast. Ropes's recognition of the fact that the interpretation of the rich as non-Christian seems to bring this passage into accord with 5:1 and in some ways to suit the context of vv. 10–11 lends some viability to the ironic proposition. He still feels, however, that it has more difficulties than the position that holds that the author is speaking heroically.[25]

We must note that most of the scholars who hold to the ironic interpretation reject the view that the rich are Christian simply because they see James using the terms "rich" and "poor" in a semireligious sense—a sense seemingly acquired in the course of history. Thus James had in mind people who are alien to the spiritual community. Because of this, the question of whether the rich are Christian or non-Christian is irrelevant and is externally imposed on the verse. "James himself does not have it in mind," says Dibelius.[26] At the same time Dibelius does point out that because "the rich" are outside the pious community, then some readers may have in mind that James is speaking of non-Christians, "but if he [James] was thinking here of Christians as well, then these are people whom he considers no longer to be included in a proper sense with Christendom"[27]—that is, they are those who no longer inwardly belong to the spiritual community.

Both the ironic as well as the heroic viewpoint, as explicated above, have a presuppositional fault. They both want to read into James the assumption that there were rich Christians in James's community (that is, rich Christians according to modern categories). The heroic viewpoint does so by artificially breaking up the antithesis of vv. 9 and 10–11 and by making the rich man a brother whose trial is the loss of his riches. In

addition, those who argue that James is speaking heroically
fail to take note of the overall view of the rich in James's
document and of the general New Testament view of the rich
in first-century Palestine—both of which were very negative.
The ironic viewpoint is able to assume that there were rich
Christians in James's community by spiritualizing the concept
of poverty. Thus, a Christian in the early church could be rich
and yet "poor," because he was "pious." This contention fails
to appreciate the social concerns of the author for his spiritual
community. Both viewpoints as explicated fail to read the
document rigorously. Instead, interpretations seem to be
created in order to placate the wealthy Christians within our
own contemporary communities.[28]

The issue of whether the rich person is a Christian or not
actually has no relevancy in this context. Nowhere in the
epistle does James make such a distinction clear. To him all
rich fall in the same category. We noted earlier that the apostle
did not have in mind two distinct communities, Jewish and
Christian, at this early period of the church—at least not as
clear a distinction as was made later. We however do feel that
James's language regarding the economically rich person has
an ironic twist—a device that is utilized to underscore the
humiliation in which the rich person lives and that is similar to
Luke's use of the rich fool (Luke 12:13–21).[29]

It should also be noted that to ask whether James is thinking
of the individual rich person or the rich as a class is also
probably to ask the wrong question.[30] James here is setting up
a contrast between the poor and the rich. The former will be
exalted and thus can truly boast.[31] The rich will be brought low
(tēi tapeinōsei), not necessarily by the loss of property and
social standing (a concept which is not spelled out in the
passage),[32] and will "fade away" (v. 11). Thus James works
with the schema humiliation–exaltation (and vice versa).[33]

A logical question to ask at this time is, How does the
author understand the schema humiliation–exaltation? Does
it have eschatological significance or some ethical signifi-

cance? Shall we interpret this schema in light of the final judgment when the fortunes of the poor will be reversed and the rich will obtain a deserved reward?[34] Or shall we interpret the reversal as something James expected presently? In this pericope the time of the reversal is not made clear, and it is possible that he had in mind a present reversal as well as an eschatological reversal.[35] To this, however, we must return when we deal with judgment on the rich.

This section (vv. 10–11) of the antithesis is descriptive (using illustrations from nature) and sets forth the sure fate of the rich. In doing this James draws on Isaiah 40:6–8, but it is not a quote in a vacuum; rather the author is quite familiar with the natural phenomena that are utilized. The imagery is that of the flowers of green herbage—a favorite image for transitoriness in Old Testament literature.[36] The phenomenon of a brief but brilliant Palestinian spring continues even to the present. The forceful picture of flowers like the anemone, cyclamen, and lily, which though profuse are gone within weeks in Palestine, truly betrays the natural, Palestinian milieu of the document. Henry G. Tristram in his *Natural History of the Bible* writes:

> Let a traveler ride over the downs of Bethlehem in February, one spangled carpet of brilliant flowers, and again in May, when all traces of verdure are gone; let him push his horse through the deep solid growth of clovers and grasses in the Valley of Jordan in the early spring, and then return and gallop across a brown, hard-baked gaping plain in June. . . . The beauty is gone, the grass is withered, the flower is faded, a brown dusty desert has supplanted a lovely garden.[37]

The manner in which the flower is portrayed as passing away demonstrates that James is not simply drawing on Old Testament imagery, but is actually acquainted with a specific phenomenon almost unique to Palestine. The author speaks of *ho helios sun tōi kausōni* as being destructive agents. It is interesting that in the lexicon of Walter Bauer, it is noted that sometimes *sun* (literally, "with") is nearly equivalent to *kai* ("and"), and James 1:11 is given as an example.[38] It seems, therefore, that *ho helios* ("the sun") and *kausōn* ("heat") are two different things. Although *kausōn* means "burning heat," here it seems to be a reference to the sirocco. It is a blasting, scorching southeast wind of the desert which blows incessantly night and day during the spring. Due to its extreme and withering dryness,[39] this hot wind is fatal to young growth and flowers. To our author, however, these flowers are not weaklings. They are being equated with the rich who seem strong and powerful. This is brought out quite clearly when reference is made to the beauty of the flower fading. The term *hē euprepeia*—which is found only here in the New Testament but is common in the LXX and classical writings—suggests "fitness to the object and its relations, and so sometimes gains a notion of stateliness or majesty, which *kalos, kallos* do not have," states Ropes.[40] Thus the imagery is more forceful and poignant, for the rich in the height of their glory and majesty are cut down.

Greater poignancy is given by the use of the aorist tense in v. 11. The aorists (as well as the future and present tenses in vv. 10–11) have usually been called "narrative" or "gnomic."[41] However, it seems that the aorist used here represents the Hebrew perfect, which is *not* used "gnomically"; rather it is used "to emphasize the suddenness and completeness of the withering."[42] Thus, the judgment upon the rich will be abrupt and final.

James goes on to indicate when the rich will "fade away" *(marainō)*; it will be *entais poreiais*. The meaning of *poreia* has long been disputed. In the New Testament the word is actually found only here and in Luke 13:22, which speaks about Christ's journey to Jerusalem.[43] The word refers basically to a journey. However, there are those who argue for a metaphorical interpretation of the word. Form critics such as Dibelius contend that if one disregards James 4:13 (which should not be called upon in a document such as James, according to Dibelius), the allusion is to one's way of life or conduct.[44] According to this argument, *poreia* is parallel to *hodos* ("way") of v. 8 and should be understood just as figuratively when referring to the experiences and fortunes of the rich. "To take it of literal journeys," says Ropes, "is wholly inappropriate to the context."[45] In this interpretation *poreia* would be equivalent to the Hebrew *derech,* which has the moral connotation of "walk," "behavior."[46] It is very interesting to note that the very scholars, like Dibelius, who argue that there is no connection between vv. 9–11 and the preceding pericope, do make an effort to parallel *poreia* in v. 11 with *hodos* in the preceding passage.

The weight of evidence, however, seems to contradict the opinion that *poreia* is used metaphorically in v. 11. In the first place, Moulton and Milligan point out that unlike *hodos, poreia* is rarely used in a metaphorical sense. They note a Greek papyrus of the second century B.C. in which *poreia* denotes a "passport" for a journey; in another papyrus dated A.D. 163 it equals a "caravan," and mention is made of camels being provided.[47] In the second place, the plural is a strong indication that the reference is to commercial travel and enterprise.[48] In the third place, one cannot ignore the parallelism with James 4:13. For example, we can note the following parallelisms: (1) *Kauchaomai* in 1:10 (implied) and in 4:16; (2) the passing away of the rich as a flower in 1:10–11 and the life of the rich which vanishes in 4:14, and so on. There is no question that chapter 4 refers to literal traveling merchants. We therefore believe that in 1:11 the allusion also is to the business travel of the rich for purposes of trade.[49]

To fully appreciate the irony of James's closing words of the pericope, and to understand the necessity of the Great Reversal, one has to describe the way trade was caried on by the rich in first-century Palestine. However, since 1:9–11 is parallel to 4:13–17, we will attempt such a description after an exegesis of the latter passage is completed.

CHAPTER 4

Favoritism and the Poor: James 2:1–13

In the second chapter of the Epistle of James we find a continuation of the author's sensitivity to the trials of the poor and his censoriousness of the rich. Unlike the other passages where the emphasis is on the condemnation of the rich, James 2:1–13 protests the actions of those who lack sensitivity to the poor and, in fact, pictures a display of prejudice on the part of some in favor of the rich. The author's illustration and contention here demonstrate that the action of those who lack sensitivity is far from "religion that is pure and true before God and the Father" (1:27). Such a religion, according to 1:27, includes the visiting of "orphans and widows in their affliction." Thus a truly religious person is "a doer that acts"—a motif that is emphasized in 1:22–27 and is illustrated in 2:1–13.[1]

It has frequently been contended that the whole epistle was written in the style of a diatribe—a style of oral discourse (utilized extensively by the Cynics) in which a dialogue is carried on with an imaginary person. This, it is argued, is particulary true of chapter 2. James is here "writing as if he were in dialogue with an audience," state proponents of this stylistic theory.[2] However, an analysis of this passage shows nothing peculiarly characteristic of the diatribe style; rather there is much that is foreign to the style.[3]

It is mainly on the basis of the stylistic argument that some exegetes determine whether *echete* ("you have") in v. 1 is interrogative or imperative. It is argued that a characteristic of the diatribe is the use of rhetorical questions; therefore, the most natural translation of the verse would see the negative *mē* as indicating a question and expecting a negative answer: 'You are not having faith in our glorious Lord Jesus Christ when you show partiality, are you?'"[4]

There are others, however, who disagree and suggest that the imperative interpretation is more in accordance with the gnomic style of the epistle and with the verses that follow 2:1.[5] Although we must admit that the meaning of the verse is not affected by whether we view *echete* as interrogative or imperative, still it is important here to note that the imperative understanding does seem to be more in keeping with the pericope as a whole. The present active imperative of *echō* ("I have") with the negative particle *mē* is a construction that prohibits the continuance of a condition or action that is existing or in progress. This construction in v. 1 indicates that the community to which the author writes is practicing the action that he is condemning; he is appealing to them to stop. We therefore should translate the construction thusly: "stop holding[6] the faith . . . *en prosōpolēmpsiais* ['with action of partiality']."[7]

The term *prosōpolēmpteō* and its cognates have been found only in Christian sources. It is a compound formed from *lambanein prosōpon* (literally "lift up the face"), the LXX translation of the Hebrew phrase *nasa' panim*. This idiomatic expression in the Old Testament had the sense of "respect of persons," with the connotation of improper partiality. We note for example Leviticus 19:15: "you shall not be partial to the poor or defer to the great." James might have had this text or similar passages (e.g., Exod. 23:1–3; Deut. 1:16, 17; 16:18–20) in mind when he used the term. Interestingly, all these passages deal with partiality to the poor in the context of a judicial setting—a point which is worth remembering when we deal later with the setting of James 2:2–3.[8]

James utilizes the phrase *en*[9] *prosōpolēmpsiais* to express the idea "with actions of partiality," that is, "showing favoritism with respect of persons."[10] In v. 1 James employs two stylistic devices to emphasize his argument. The first is a syntactical device: "in partiality" stands emphatically after the negative *mē*. The second is that he employs the plural, thus giving the impression that there had been several manifestations or varied forms of partiality practiced in the community.[11]

The question of the type of genitive in the phrase *tēn pistin*[12] *tou kuriou hēmōn Iēsou Christou tés doxēs* has long been a thorny one. Because this genitive qualifier is unusual, some commentators have regarded the *tou kuriou hēmōn* as a later interpolation.[13] This, however, is an extreme solution. In the first place, there are two main possibilities for translating the phrase *pistin . . . Iēsou Christou,* a subjective translation: "the faith *of* our Lord Jesus Christ," or an objective translation: "faith *in* our Lord Jesus Christ." Hort interestingly notes that "the former is not a likely sense to be meant without some special indication of it: the latter is not supported by any clear parallels, and (taken thus nakedly) gives a not very relevant turn to the sentence."[14] However, a majority of scholars have held the opinion that the genitive here—and always in the phrase *pistis Iēsou Christou*—is an objective genitive, that is, the faith or trust which the believer places in Christ. That particular viewpoint is based on the interpretation of texts— especially Romans 3:22 and Galations 2:16[15]—that, it is argued, support the objective interpretation. In opposition to that position, a few scholars, arguing particularly from the Galatian passage, have found difficulties with the objective interpretation and have opted for a subjective one.[16] In most of the cases, they say, the "faith of Christ" is understood as the faithful obedience of Christ.[17] If this be the case, James's audience need not be those professing faith *in* Christ, that is believers, but could be those who possess the quality of faith like that which Christ demonstrated. We must admit that the use of the genitive in James is not as clear as it might seem to be in the Pauline corpus. It seems to us that it is because of this difficulty that Hort sees the phrase as "more comprehensive" than merely "objective" or "subjective." He writes that the phrase

> answers to an idea widely spread in the NT; [it refers to a faith] "which comes from Him, and depends on Him," "the faith which He taught, and makes possible, and bestows": it is a faith in God, enlarged and strengthened by the revelation of His Son; the faith in God which specially arises out of the Gospel and rests on Him of whom the Gospel speaks. It thus *includes* a faith *in* Christ: but this is only the first step on the way to a surer and better faith in God.[18]

Thus for Hort the phrase includes elements of both the objective and subjective interpretations. The problem here, however, is that neither Hort's view nor the exclusively objective or exclusively subjective interpretation is made clear in James. James does not deal with the issue as extensively as Paul—particularly he does not deal with the theological meaning of *pistis Christou*. Besides, we do not believe James is in any dialogue with Paul in this chapter.[19] Thus we cannot use Paul's understanding of *pistis Christou* to interpret James. It seems that the wiser approach would be not to attempt a specific interpretation of the genitive, but just to grasp the basic contention of the author: prejudice and faith (whether it be of or in Christ) are incompatible; therefore, partiality must stop.

The difficulty of the verse does not end with the phrase just discussed; it comes to a climax with the odd phrase *tēs doxēs*. So difficult is the later phrase that Elliot-Binns has suggested that " 'Jesus Christ,' or perhaps 'the Lord of Glory,' may have been a marginal gloss."[20] Others have proposed numerous interpretations.[21] Two of these seem to deserve mention. First, Adamson proposes that "glory" must be closely connected with the name of Christ, "possibly as a title in apposition."[22] He also suggests that *hēmōn* ("our") be transfered to the end of the sentence, making Christ "our glory."[23] Taking *tēs doxēs* in apposition may be correct, but the suggestion of transferring *hēmōn* has little support.[24]

The second suggested interpretation that deserves mention is that proposed by scholars such as Ropes, Dibelius, and Davids.[25] They see the genitive as a qualitative genitive,[26] and therefore translate the phrase, "our glorious Lord Jesus." Adamson feels that this interpretation is arbitrary.[27] Yet neither the "Christ our glory" nor the "our glorious Lord Jesus" is contrary to the intent of the passage. For in these lines James is contrasting the discrimination against the poor in favor of the rich with the glory which Christ is and in which Christ dwells. It may be correct to identify the *doxē* with the Shekinah,[28] seeing James as arising out of an intensely Jewish milieu. Therefore, the key question that arises in the passage becomes: How can one pay special regard to those who possess only a counterfeit glory when compared with the glory of the Shekinah?[29]

James connects v. 1 with the following verses by *gar* ("for") in an effort to illustrate the problems of partiality. Immediately in v. 2 we find a problem. The author uses *ean* with the aorist subjunctive and thus creates a third class condition in the subjunctive mood. The question therefore arises whether he intends the illustration of vv. 2–4 to be hypothetical or whether he is relating an actual incident. There are those who contend that the case mentioned in the verses was one that James heard about—an incident in a Jewish synagogue that believers from Israel still visited.[30]

There seems to be a strong case, however, for arguing that the incident was hypothetical. Those who postulate the diatribe style theory are the strongest proponents of this view. The example in these verses is seen as characteristic of the rhetorical style of the diatribe.[31] Thus Dibelius states emphatically that this example which is related for a paraenetic purpose cannot be used as a historical source for actual circumstance within the Christian communities. . . . Such a use of Jas. 2:2ff is based upon a method of interpretation which is not appropriate given the literary character of Jas.[32]

Scholars like Dibelius and those who follow his line argue that because the illustration is not based on an actual incident, consideration of the community or the social situation out of which it grew is irrelevant. This of course is a logical stance for these proponents, seeing as they are working with the assumption that James "spiritualizes" the rich and poor—that in James rich = pious. In other words, because it seems quite evident that the illustration here refers to literal economics and class distinction, it is necessary for scholars like Dibelius to suggest that the case is a "constructed" illustration.

If these verses were merely a paraenetic example without any concern for reality, a pertinent question would be: "How effective would this example be if it were completely unrelated to the experience of the readers?"[33] After considering that question, one tends to feel that the example could not have been divorced from the local conditions within the community of the author.[34] At the same time, we recognize that the grammatical structure seems to prevent one from historicizing the incident and, thus, it is possible to take it as a hypothetical case. It is possible that it is a typical or composite incident. What is necessary is that we find the meaning of the example, and to do that we must understand the type of situation being depicted.[35]

It would seem that the most ideal key toward an understanding of the situation of this illustration might lie in the use of the word *sunagōge*. It has been argued that the use of the term here is an incidental argument for an early date of the document and tends to confirm the opinion that James is writing out of his own Palestinian experiences.[36] It has been suggested that the procedures described in v. 3 regarding sitting and standing "here" *(ōde)* and "there" *(ekei)* are typical of a specific earlier type of synagogue worship, particularly popular in Palestine.[37] This interpretation has, however, been questioned, because some feel it places too great an emphasis on *ōde* and *ekei*. "These words," contends Dibelius, "may say nothing more than that in one case the guest is led to a comfortable seat, while the other guest is given merely some lazy gesture: 'Over there is a place.' "[38] In addition, he contends that it is precarious to conclude from the use of *sunagōge* anything about the time and place of the incident.[39]

Another problem arises in regard to the word *sunagōge:* Does it refer to an assembly or to a building? Some argue that it probably means the former.[40] We must recognize, however, that this Greek word is a translation of the Hebrew *'edah,* which refers to a building as well as to an assembly or community and is translated in the LXX as both *sunagōgue* and *ekklēsia*.[41] Interestingly, James uses both terms in the epistle. In 5:14 the term *ekklēsia* is generally accepted to refer to the community. Thus when James uses *sunagōge* in chapter 2 of his epistle it would seem that he wishes to emphasize primarily the place of meeting.[42] It is possible that both meanings are intended in this passage,[43] but it seems reasonable to conclude that James's primary emphasis is on the physical structure.

The fact that the author refers to the synagogue as *sunagōgue humōn* ("our synagogue") would seem to prohibit the supposition that Jewish synagogue is meant, that is, if one takes the document as being addressed exclusively to a Christian community. This view is held by a number of commentators who feel that the place being designated is a separate place of worship under Christian direction but that when James refers to it he still utilizes the old nomenclature.[44] Because Christians had no church buildings at this period, Moffatt conjectures that the place is some large room in the house of a wealthy member or a hall hired for the purpose of a meeting, as in Acts 19:1.[45]

Such an argument is based on the presupposition that the document is primarily or exclusively addressed to Christians. Furthermore, such a view does not take into consideration the early Palestinian Judeo-Christian millieu out of which the epistle arose. It seems more appropriate to view the term in its Jewish context and to understand the illustration as a scene being enacted in a Jewish synagogue which both Christians and non-Christian Jews attended in the early years of Palestinian Christianity.[46]

The question as to the setting being depicted in these verses is a perplexing one. Traditionally the view has been that the scene portrayed is a worship setting. One of the arguments for this opinion is based on the following statements in v. 3: " 'Have a seat here please,' . . ."[47] 'Stand there,' or, 'Sit at my feet' " (RSV). It is argued that the Jews had a custom of having distinguished places in the synagogue. Evidence is brought forth such as Jesus' sayings in Matthew 26:6, Mark 12:39, Luke 11:43 and 2:46, in which he denounces the Scribes and Pharisees who love the best seats in the synagogues.[48] It is also noted that "the seats most coveted among the Jews were those near the end of the synagogue which looked towards Jerusalem, and at which stood the ark that contained the sacred roll of the Law."[49] Gaster, in the original English edition of *The Dead Sea Scriptures,* states that the Hebrew and Aramaic word for "seat" also has the nuance of "status." Furthermore, the idiom "to stand without" was a common Hebrew expression for "to be excluded from society." Gaster therefore suggests that James "is echoing this injunction, and not referring specifically to the seating arrangements in a synagogue."[50] It is not clear that James here is utilizing such a Hebrew idiom; rather, we think he is dealing with actual seating in a synagogue setting.

The worship setting, however, has been challenged. The Jewish synagogues were used not only for cultic rites but also for the transaction of business.[51] Josephus, the first-century

Jewish historian, reports that during the war against Rome meetings of a political character were held on the Sabbath and subsequent days in what was possibly a great synagogue in Tiberias.[52] Rabbi Johanan also gave permission for persons to "go to synagogues and to school houses to watch over public affairs on Sabbath."[53]

It seems unlikely that the setting being portrayed here is a political gathering or a meeting for a business transaction. It is more probable that the scene is a judicial one. Campegius Vitringa in the seventeenth century pointed out that petty courts of judicature were held in synagogues,[54] and more recently scholars such as Adam Clarke[55] and Roy Bowen Ward[56] have argued for a judicial setting in James 2. It is interesting to note here that in the nineteenth century F. C. Cook noted that in some cases the officers in the synagogues had judicial functions, but he disagrees that the synagogue referred to in James 2 is a judicial setting. Cook, by the way, goes on totally to misread James's thrust, which rules out *all* partiality in or out of a cultic setting, when he adds that "the rebuke implies that 'rich and poor were meeting together' not as members of a Society in which *such distinctions must be recognized*[!], but as in the presence of 'the Maker of them all,' before whom they are absolutely equal" (emphasis added).[57]

The fact that the synagogues were used as places for judicial proceedings seems to be attested to by the New Testament and confirmed by the Rabbinic literature. The New Testament documents speak of flogging in the synagogues (Matt. 10:17; 23:34; Mark 13:9; Acts 26:11), which implies that a case had been judicially dealt with prior to the punishment. Furthermore, the statement of Jesus, "when they bring you before the synagogue . . . do not be anxious how or what you are to answer or what you are to say" (Luke 12:11; see 21:12), suggests a legal proceeding. The Babylonian Talmud also reports a divorce case which came before Rabbi Johanan at the synagogue of Caesarea,[58] and in the same synagogue the Jerusalem Talmud records that Abbahu, the head of the school of Caesarea (in the fourth century), decided questions of law.[59] It is quite possible that the autonomous courts that were scattered throughout Palestine and that were composed of three judges to decide cases concerning property[60] were convened in the synagogues. Interestingly, these courts were in a number of cases usurped by a wealthy landowner who would proclaim himself the sole judge[61] and who would gain the reputation of handing down oppressive judgments.[62]

The case for James 2 to be read against a judicial background becomes very strong when we compare the illustration with two descriptions for a Rabbinic text. The first deals with two persons coming to court, one in rags and the other well dressed: "How do we know that, if two come to court, one clothed in rags and the other in fine raiment worth a hundred *manehs,* they [the court] should say to him [the well dressed man], Either dress like him, or dress him like you'? "[63] The second deals with the matter of sitting and standing in court (it should be noted that in litigation the judges sit and the litigants stand):

> Rabbah son of R. Huna said: If a Rabbinical scholar and an illiterate person have some dispute with each other, and come to court, we persuade the Rabbinical scholar to sit; and to the illiterate person we also say, "Sit," and if he stands, it matters not. Rab son of R. Sherabya had a case before R. Papa. He told him to sit, and told his opponent also to sit; but the attendant of the court came and nudged [literally "kicked," according to the footnote in the Talmud] the illiterate man and made him stand up.[64]

The similarities of these two descriptions with James 2:2-3 are very striking. Verse 2 of the passage in James deals with two persons, one with gold rings and in fine clothing, the other poor and shabbily clothed. This is quite parallel to the one clothed in rags and the other in fine raiment in the Talmudic text. In v. 3 of James 2 we see the wealthy person being given a seat while the poor one is told to stand—a practice forbidden by the Rabbinic judge but, interestingly, practiced by the court attendant in the Rabbinic text.

Roy Bowen Ward argues very strongly that when we read the passage in James against such judicial background, it becomes more intelligible, and, therefore, it should be understood as follows:

> If there should come before your judicial assembly a richly dressed man and a poor man in rags, and if you should favor the richly clad man by allowing him to sit while you make the poor man stand (or even worse, if you tell him to sit down at "the footstool of my feet"), have you not practiced partiality among yourselves and become unjust judges?[65]

It is interesting to note that Ward sees the judicial interpretation as the answer to Dibelius's problem with regards to *ptōchos* ("poor") in this passage. As noted before, Dibelius argues that James had taken over the concept of the evil rich and the pious poor from Judaism—that is, in James the rich are outside the pious community, while the term "poor" indicates members of the community. In James 2, however, both who enter are strangers, even the *ptōchos*. Dibelius solves the problem by arguing that this is just a paraenetic example—not a historical account—and that James had in mind only the antithesis "rich/poor," not "believer/nonbeliever."[66] Ward also argues for the *anawin*-piety interpretation throughout James but believes that the author is consistent in James 2 and that the passage need not merely be read as a paraenetic example. Ward writes, "When the example is read as one informed by judicial tradition, the man described as *ptōchos* would be assumed to be a member who comes to a judicial assembly."[67]

The passage, however, does not clearly demonstrate that the concern is with "member and nonmember." Nor is there anything in the illustration to indicate that James is dealing with poverty in a pietistic sense. Furthermore, if the illustration is an adaptation of the judicial one in the Rabbinic text cited above (and there is much reason to believe it is—though we must not ignore the possibility that the same actions could take place in a worship setting), it is clear that James is drawing a vivid illustration in which the categories "rich and poor" are understood more in their sociological sense than religiously. It seems clear, therefore, that the author is interested in the sociological antithesis rich/poor, with emphasis on the partiality shown to the former.

James clearly distinguishes the type of rich person about whom he is speaking. Instead of merely referring to him as "the rich," he writes "a man in gold rings in fine clothing"—characteristic adornment of a wealthy person. At this point it is worthwhile noting the three groups into which one can classify the wealthy (from the point of view of the economic basis of their wealth) in the New Testament and particularly in James. The first are the landowners and agriculturalists. These are addressed in James 5. The second are the merchants. James 4:14–17 deals with this group. The third group deals directly with money. James 2, particularly v. 6, speaks about these financiers. In the illustration in James 2, however, a person from any one of these groups could be the focus of attention.

Not all feel that the "ring" and "fine clothing" in v. 2 refer to the economic reality of the person being depicted. It is suggested that the ring indicates that the person had senatorial rank or was a Roman nobleman or politician, for during the early days of the Roman Empire only persons of that rank could wear a gold ring. Furthermore, it is suggested that the person was seeking political office and adherents, for a *toga candida* was worn by candidates for elective office. Therefore, the visitor mentioned in James is likely to be a canvassing politician.[68]

That argument, however, seems to be disproved by the

ancient documents. We note, for example (although these could possibly be exceptional cases) the following instances: Juvenal speaks of Crispinus, a slave-born citizen of a city in the Nile Delta, who "airs a summer ring of gold on his sweating finger";[69] Martial writes of one Charinus who wears six rings on each of his fingers and never takes them off "at night nor when he bathes";[70] Epictetus, who wrote late in the first and early in the second century A.D. speaks of a white-haired old man with many gold rings on his fingers.[71] Epictetus says nothing of the man's station in life, but the context of the discourse does not give the impression that the old man is a politician.

Another interesting interpretation is that the rich person depicted in James 2 is of Roman equestrian status. The person would not necessarily belong to the "metropolitan aristocracy," but rather James "is thinking in terms of the big businessmen of the eastern cities."[72] Although it is correct that Hellenistic politics is not involved in the passage and that only a Palestinian situation is being depicted,[73] that does not necessarily mean that, working by elimination, the person illustrated in the passage need be of Roman equestrian status. The custom of wearing rings and fine clothing[74] was popular through the empire and was practiced in Palestine.[75] Throughout the empire there was a wanton display of wealth on every hand: "Upon the streets men and women appeared robed in fine raiment and bedecked with gold ornaments and precious gems."[76] The extravagances of the rich of the empire were found in Jerusalem—in the houses, clothing, servants, and rich offerings of the wealthy.[77]

James, therefore, is referring to the wealthy in Palestine and is using two outstanding features of their wealth (the gold rings and fine clothing) to characterize the person depicted. The emphasis of the author in James 2, however, is on the fact that his readers have conceded superiority to the rich, vis-à-vis the poor, thus making "a distinction, a differentiation"[78] in favor of the rich and, in that way, are "judges of evil reasoning." It is worthwhile noting that the concept of "judges" in v. 4 makes much more sense if the illustration in vv. 2 and 3 is interpreted as being informed by the judicial tradition.[79]

In v. 5 we find a new development of thought. Whether there is a connection with the preceding text is a matter of debate. It is suggested that vv. 5–7 break the connection between vv. 2–4 and 8–13 and should be ascribed therefore to a Christian editor who introduced the verses "in order to adapt the Jewish original of vv. 1–4, 8–13 to Christian conditions."[80] However, this adaptation is not necessary, for vv. 5–7 do not break the link between vv. 2–4 and 8–13: what happens is that since the illustration in 2–4 is now complete, the author proceeds to develop his sensitivity to the poor and his censoriousness of the rich and those who show favoritism to them— the very reverse of the attitude of those in the illustration. Verses 5–13 make three points that develop the illustration in vv.2–4: (1) the election of the poor by God; (2) the oppression of the poor by the rich; and (3) the condemnation of those transgressors of the law who show partiality to the rich.

1. The initial question we must pose in reference to the first point is: What type of dative is used in the phrase *tous ptochous tōi kosmōi?* Two possibilities have been proposed: a dative of respect—"those poor in worldly goods"; or a dative of advantage—"those who are poor before the world."[81] In the first, *tōi kosmōi* would be taken as naming the possessions which the poor lack. But we must note that the poor lack not the world but the goods of the world.[82] A number of scholars consider the second the more likely possiblity, for *plousious en pistei* does not mean "rich with regard to faith," rather the meaning should be "rich in that sphere which is called 'faith'," a phrase that emphasizes how the world views faith. Therefore, *potchous tōi kosmōi* should be understood accordingly—as "poor before the world." Thus Dibelius, for example, sees "in faith" forming an antithesis to "before the world."[83] James, these scholars argue, is saying that faith is a

matter of denying (being poor in) the world. Poverty becomes a religious category.

However, contrary to the two possibilities discussed above, it would seem that because James is dealing with the literal poor here, and not strictly with a religious nuance as is widely advocated,[84] the dative should be seen as a local dative of place—it is the economic poor who are spatially in the world. In support of this we could compare the similar phrase in Matthew 5:3. Interestingly, Moule in his *An Idiom Book* seems to contrast the phrases, for he asks "Does *hoi ptōchoi tōi pneumati* . . . mean *'the poor' used in its spiritual* (i.e., *religious) connotation,* while *tous ptōchous tōi kosmōi,* Jas. 2:5, means *the literally, i.e. materially, poor?*"[85] However, if we are correct in our contention that the phrase in Matthew deals with the materially poor, especially in the spiritual realm of the community (a spatial idea), then we should so interpret James. Rather than limiting his concerns to any particular community like Matthew's or the Qumran community, he is speaking in general terms of the literal poor in the world. The emphasis in the verse, however, is not the present station of the poor in this world, but the purpose for which they are chosen—namely, that they might be rich in the sphere which is called faith[86] and be inheritors of the kingdom. We must note here that James does not develop such themes as "the kingdom"; therefore, it is difficult to know what he means by the use of the term. It is possible that the kingdom referred to here is the future kingdom, as is possibly indicated by the word *epēngeilato* ("he promised").[87]

This verse poses a problem especially in Christian communities where there are many wealthy members. Is there a doctrine of election being taught here—a doctrine which excludes all rich from final salvation or even the experience of faith? Some have attempted to solve the problem by noting that the election of the poor is not "due to any merit of their poverty, but in fact, poverty and election coincide." The rich are then placated with an assurance such as "this does not deny that an occasional rich man may have become a christian."[88]

Such an addendum does not seem to be in the mind of the writer. For him the rich are outside the sphere of salvation and faith. In this James shows much affinity with Luke—especially in his beatitudes, where blessings are only for the poor and woes are pronounced upon the rich. Thus, we question Frank Stagg's suggestion that James "thought of piety as belonging *more* to the poor than to the rich."[89] Rather he thought of piety as belonging *only* to the poor. Stagg is correct, however, in noting that "eudaemonism, the vulgar idea that one's wealth is a sign of divine favor, is rejected by Jesus and James."[90] We must read James rigorously without imposing contemporary concerns upon the book and its author. We must recognize that James stands with the tradition of the very primitive church—a church which saw its mission as being to the poor (Luke 4:18), the chosen of God.

2. The rich seem to be rejected of God because of what they do. Their actions, which are the subject of vv. 6 and 7, are three-fold: they oppress; they take court action; they blaspheme. There is generally no question among interpreters as to the type of oppression being referred to in v. 6. Even Dibelius admits that it "brings to mind social oppression."[91] The fact that the oppression here is social is even more evident when it is realized that James adopts the word *katadunasteuō* ("oppress") from the LXX—a term the prophets were famous for using in their denunciation of social injustice committed by the rich against the poor, widows, and orphans.[92] The term is very strong and has violent, physical overtones, with the emphasis on exploitation and domination.[93] It is also significant that in the only other place the word is used in the New Testament, the "devil" is the subject (Acts 10:38).

This physical oppression led to the poor being dragged into court by the rich. The impression one gets is that this legal action was over such issues as debts, rents, wages, and pledges.[94] Paul Furfey agrees that the injustice here contemplated seems to be of a financial character. Suggesting that it is possibly usury, he notes:

> The lending of money at interest was prohibited among Israelites by the Mosaic Code, but the foreigner [Deut. 23:21] was not protected by this provision. . . . It may be that avaricious Jews made their conversion to Christianity an excuse to circumvent the regulation, in which case, however, the *kritēria* before which the unfortunate brethren were brought could hardly have been Jewish tribunals. . . . The passage from James suggests rather obscurely the activities of Jewish bankers.[95]

It is unlikely that usury is the issue at hand, for it is very doubtful that we can make a distinction between Jews and Jewish Christians in the period of the epistle. However, the problem does seem to be financial, and Jewish bankers (if we may so refer to them) seem to be at the heart of it. Now we must be careful not to draw too sharp a distinction among bankers, rich agriculturalists, or even merchants, for, as will be seen later, in the majority of cases a rich person was a large landowner, merchant, and banker all at the same time. In this case our author seems to be referring to the specific financial aspect of the oppression which resulted in physically dragging the poor into court because of their debts—such action made all the more possible because of the prosbul promulgated by Hillel which allowed a creditor to collect debts during the Sabbatical Year. James is here, therefore, a Shammaite.

The third reason for the rejection of the rich is that they blaspheme. Now what does the author mean by "they blaspheme the good name which is called over you"? Again we have a phrase without any context or an explication of its meaning. What we do know is that the first aorist passive of *epikaleō* ("called over") with *onoma* ("name"), as used here, indicates that the one over whom the name is invoked is the property of the one with the name.[96] For those who hold to the opinion that the community to which James is writing is an exclusively Christian one, the solution to the problem is simply that the name refers either to "Christ," "Christians," or "Jesus." There are a number of problems with this opinion, however. First, there is no evidence that either the name of Jesus Christ or the title "Christians" was invoked over the members of the community.[97] Second, it is questionable whether the adjective *to kalon* ("good") has reference to those titles. Third, our argument still stands: James probably is not writing to an exclusively Christian community.

It seems more likely that the author again is utilizing an Old Testament formula and is alluding to the special name of God, Yahweh—this is indicated by the adjective *kalōs*. In a number of Old Testament texts (as well as in Acts 15:17, which quotes the Old Testament) people and places are called by Yahweh's name and are thus Yahweh's property (Kings 8:43; Jer. 7:30; 14:9, etc.). With this interpretation, it seems clear that the "poor being chosen of God" and the "invoking of the good name" as an indication of possession stand in parallelism.

It is also possible that James had in mind the passage in 1 Enoch which condemns the rich for their unrighteousness and oppression. In the midst of the woes pronounced upon them we find a very interesting bicolon by the author of the Book of Enoch:

> You have not remembered the Most High in the days of
> your riches;
> You have committed blasphemy and unrighteousness
> [94:8-9].

The possibility that James is drawing upon this passage (even partially) is even more evident when we recognize that he draws upon it again in the diatribe against the rich in chapter 5. We must realize, however, that the important point of James is that (whatever the meaning of "the good name") one has no right to show favors to a class of blasphemers, and to oppress the poor, God's chosen possession, is actually to blaspheme.

3. In vv. 8–13 James makes a third point about the development and explication of the illustration in vv. 2–4. It is obvious that vv. 8–13 are part of the argument because James uses the conjunction *mentoi,* which points to a specific connection with the preceding verses.[98] The particle has the force of a strong affirmation and should be translated "if you really."[99] Thus, "the force of the particle seems to lie in an implied reference to a contradiction between the respect of persons and . . . fulfillment of the law."[100] It is impossible to conduct oneself in the manner represented in the illustration and claim to be fulfilling the law.

This claim, however, seems to have been made by those who were catering exclusively to the rich. It is possible that they were using this "law"[101] as an excuse for honoring the rich— that is, by attending to the rich they were showing love to their neighbor. James might be replying to this argument.[102] To love one's neighbor is good, but showing partiality is not a fulfillment of the law. On the contrary, those who discriminate against the poor "work sin" *(harmartian ergaxesthe)* and are convicted as "transgressors" *(parabatēs)* of the law. Significantly, James links such partiality with such sins as murder and adultery (v. 11)—an indication of how heinous the crime of discrimination against the poor is to James. Furthermore, the use of the participle *elegchomenoi* ("convicted") in v. 9 indicates that the sin of partiality is against the whole law, not just a single commandment.[103] It is in this context that James writes (in v. 10) that "whoever keeps the whole law, but fails in one point [that point in this context being partiality] has become guilty of all of it." And it is also in this connection that v. 13 is presented. Those who discriminate against the poor are breakers of the law because they have failed to show mercy. To such there will be no mercy in the judgment.[104]

According to James, then, anyone who honors the rich at the expense of the poor discriminates against those whom God has elected; shows favor to those who oppress God's chosen— as well as blaspheming God whose possession the poor are; and transgresses the whole law of God and is, therefore, in the same category as the murderer and adulterer. That one can expect no mercy in the judgment.[105]

CHAPTER 5

The Merchant Class and the Poor:
James 4:13–17

Beginning with 4:13, James commences his final attack on the rich. That this is the commencement of the final diatribe against the wealthy is not universally accepted, however. Therefore various opinions about the connection of 4:13–17 with 5:1–6 (or with what precedes it) are proposed. It is argued that 4:13–17 is an independent section.[1] Some say that we should view the passages not as parallel but in terms of the second pericope being developed from the first.[2] Others contend that the classes rebuked in both passages are distinct.[3] Finally, some state that the rebuked classes are the same.[4]

What is clear at this point is that both passages have the identical mode of introduction—*age nun*. Furthermore, careful reading of both passages gives the impression that the ideas are parallel.[5] Of course the persons in 4:13–17 (unlike those in chap. 5) are not called by name, but are referred to only as *hoi legontes* ("those who say"). This designation exactly expresses the leading thought of the pericope, and it is "through their thinking they are branded": yet it has been further noted that "the characterization in 4:13ff requires nothing short of the characterization *expresis verbis* in 5:1 as *hoi plousioi* ["the rich"]."[6]

It must be remembered that the epistle is dealing with the three groups of rich persons specifically mentioned in the New Testament: in chapter 2 James seems to be referring to financiers; in 4:13–17 he has in mind the merchants; and in 5:1–6 James is writing about the rich agriculturalists.[7] However, we must realize that these "classes" are not distinct; rather, the activities are different functions of the same individual or individuals. What James is doing in this final outburst in 4:13–17 and 5:1–6 is attacking the rich from the perspective of two of their functions in the economic sphere. Both passages, therefore, should be read as a unit. In this work we will do that, although our discussion will be divided into two chapters.

The connection of 4:13–5:6 with the preceding series of imperatives is problematic. Form critics, of course, view the section as independent of the preceding verses, noting that the abrupt change from v. 12 to v. 13 is characteristic of paraenesis.[8] Others try to find a connection. For example it is suggested that 4:13–17 possibly depicts a further example of the sins of the tongue discussed in the preceding verses, though it is felt that "any real connection with what precedes is so tenuous that this section is practically independent."[9] On the other hand, a more confident proposal states that the connection lies in the weakness and ignorance of those James discusses in the two sections: "The thought of his weakness and ignorance should deter man from judging his fellows and finding fault with the law: it should also prevent him from making confident assertions to the future."[10] That this is the connection seems dubious to us, however, and we must admit that finding a direct connection is a difficult proposition. Our suggestion is that in 4:13–5:6 James is making the concluding remarks of the overall position of the epistle toward the rich and poor—he summarizes and strengthens what he has said before. He further gives comfort to the "suffering community" by further explicating the final judgment on the rich.

James begins his final onslaught with the attention-arresting *age nun* (literally "go now"). We agree with a number of other exegetes that *age* as used in 4:13 has its usual insistent (and, here, a somewhat brusque) nuance as a form of address, while *nun* increases the insistency.[11] A contrary opinion states that the phrase is a Hellenistic coloquial expression that is not as harsh as the traditional nuance. This opinion finds the New English Bible translation, " 'A word with you, you who say . . .,' more appropriate because the address is not argumentative but friendly."[12] Harold Songer, who proposes such an understanding of the text, sees the persons being addressed not as bad or evil persons but as

> industrious and ambitious small businessmen of the first century who are courageously planning future operations as travelling traders. . . . James is not objecting to their planning nor their desire for profit, but seeking to stress that men need to be aware of the reality of God and to consider him in their deliberations.[13]

This interpretation and that of the New English Bible read a modern situation into the biblical thought. Interestingly enough, the New English Bible translates *age nun* in 5:1 as "next a word to you." Yet the contents of the pericope that follows definitely show that the address there is not friendly in the least. On the contrary, James is delivering a denunciation in the style of a prophetic diatribe—not a friendly dialogue at all. A careful comparison with other prophetic utterances demonstrates that the style and characteristic of the material are similar to a familiar pattern in the scriptures. It is therefore difficult to escape the strong impression that James is modeling his utterance on the prophetic pronouncements of doom—for example, Isaiah 5:8: "Woe to those who join house to house . . ."; 1 Enoch 94:6–95:7; Luke 6:24: "But woe to you that are rich . . ."; and Revelation 18:11–19:23.[14]

This vigorous attack, signaled by the *age nun,* is leveled at the "businessmen" (rather than the "landed proprietors" of chap. 5),[15] "the godless merchants,"[16] "the commercial schemers,"[17] those involved in "the restless activity of commercial enterprise."[18] The picture here is not of people who run small businesses—not of the little shopkeeper of Jerusalem, Antioch, or any similar city or town. Rather it is of the rich trader, as is suggested by the word *emporeusometha* ("we will go")[19]—a word that occurs only one other place in the New Testament where it means "to cheat or deceive" (2 Pet. 2:3). As Alexander Ross notes, the word "is an eloquent commentary on the cheating which too often attended ancient trading."[20]

The passage, then, is aimed at the arrogant merchant: "The skillful use of the repetitive *we will go . . . and stay . . . and make a profit,* and the mention of the year's stay, both suggest deliberate and calculated arrogance."[21] The persons James refers to were the type of schemers who would do what they liked, go where they liked, and remain as long as they liked.

To better understand the passages—1:10–11 and 4:13–17— in which James attacks those engaged in business pursuits, we need to understand travel for such purposes and describe such enterprises in the first century, particularly in Syro-Palestine. Hellenistic economics and the way of life of former centuries, however, influenced the social structure of the period about which James writes. Therefore it would be worthwhile to take a brief look at the pre-Roman era; that would help us somewhat to comprehend the situation in the period under discussion.

International travel during the pre-Roman period was common. It was made particularly attractive (whether to the merchant, prospective colonist, or tourist) by the geographical treatises which were easily accessible to almost everyone. Thus a merchant could plan a voyage, choose a route, and draw up an itinerary by consulting the best and latest *periploi* and *periodoi.* Merchants like those mentioned by James could easily plan their voyages with a knowledge of which territories were more attractive and offered the better prospects for exploitation.[22]

Much of the travel during the pre-Roman period was by sea. The voyages were neither fast, nor comfortable, nor safe. Due to the slowness of the voyages, merchants had to plan for lengthy business trips. Sea travel was slow because ships hugged the coast and made frequent stops for repairs and replenishment of supplies of water and provisions. Merchants took these stops as an opportunity to trade and carry on their commercial enterprising, for behind these harbors were seaports where merchants spent many days trading.[23] This type of adventure seems to have brought in much gain for the entrepreneur. It is probable that Julianus of Egypt had this in mind when he wrote that "sea voyages give profit."[24]

It should not be thought that James's thought was limited to maritime enterprising, and thus it is helpful to describe briefly land travel in the pre-Roman period. Land travel was common, but it was often slow and unsafe. Swift journeys were, however, possible for the wealthy who rode on horseback or in horse-drawn carriages. The big businessperson or merchant could reach a town or city of business relatively quickly and thus do greater business. The poor usually traveled much more slowly, using the slower donkeys and mules, and often traveled in caravans for safety sake.[25] Whatever the mode of travel and transportation, export trade and all types of commercial activities were enhanced, particularly for the wealthy merchants, by trade routes which were developed.

The social and economic heritage of the Hellenistic world was transmitted to the Roman Empire. Syro-Palestine was one of the areas in which certain features of Hellenistic social and economic life developed most prominently, and its economic capacities improved under Roman rule. New cities and towns were built. Communication was improved with the development of new trade routes, harbors, and warehouses (for example, those built by Herod and his family), all of which did much for trade.[26] In addition to those developments, mines, quarries, smelteries, and food-processing facilities were built. They not only enhanced trade and commerce, but also increased the level of economic exploitation.[27]

Although travel remained slow during the Roman period, the ease and safety of travel were improved considerably. Thus the period was referred to as the "halcyon days" for travelers.[28] This was brought about by the unification of the empire, the ensuing peace, and the protection of the communication routes by the emperor's naval patrol squadrons and imperial police force.[29]

A second factor that brought palmy days for the merchant was the road system. An increasing number of well-paved roads, though built especially for military purposes, were used for commercial activities.[30] Paved roads increased the speed of travel.[31] These improved road systems as well as sea travel gradually opened new markets in many Roman provinces and gave the merchant access to all the major trade centers.[32]

It is obvious, then, why it was relatively easy for a merchant to go from city to city or port to port "to trade and get gain" and gather great wealth. Although the picture of commercial activities throughout the empire fits James's statement about a merchant who says he is going to go "into such and such a town and spend a year there and trade and get gain," yet it seems more likely that his denunciations are aimed more specifically at merchants closer to his sphere of influence—namely, Syro-Palestine.[33] What type of trade and commercial undertaking were prevalent throughout that region and could have informed James's thought?

Syria was important to the Roman Empire, especially because of its position as a center for trade and industry. For many centuries Syria was famous for its merchants and the trafficking of raw materials. The prophet Ezekiel lamented over Tyre (one of its main cities) and spoke of it as one "who dwells at the entrance to the sea, merchant of the peoples on many coastlands. . . ." (Ezek. 27:3). It seems to be true that from earliest times "few races show such an instinct for trade as the Syrians."[34]

The position of Syria was ideal for good communication between north and south, east and west—as a converging spot for the major trade routes from every direction. Damascus, for example, formed a natural trade center "where the riches from every land of the old world could be exchanged."[35] The fact that Paul (in Acts 21) could embark on a vessel which made frequent calls at small havens shows that along the whole length of the coast of Syria a busy commerce was kept up.[36]

Though Syria's overall mineral resources were poor, its agricultural wealth was great. Not only did its timber from the Lebanese forests provide for great trade, but its corn, cereal, fruit trees, and scented plants made it famous. It is claimed that Antioch—among other of Syria's cities—was second to none in "wealth and gaiety which it displayed by day, or by night, when its streets were ablaze with artificial lights."[37] Residing in Antioch were opulent merchant shippers of the Orient who "lived a life of ostentatious luxury."[38] This luxurious living, however, was limited to a small section of the population—evident in Chrysostom's statement (if we accept Rostovtzeff's suggstion that fourth-century Antioch was not much different from first-century Antioch[39]): "A tenth part is of the rich, and a tenth of the poor that have nothing at all, and the rest of a middle sort."[40] Chrysostom describes the typical rich men of the city as having many acres of land, ten or twenty or even more houses, as many baths, one or two thousand slaves, and chariots fastened with silver and overlaid with gold.[41] This quality of living was possible because the city was a great center of commerce and transportation.

Throughout the Palestinian regions of Judea, Samaria, and Galilee, commercial activities were also on the upswing during Roman rule. Palestine was a great land-bridge between Asia to the east and Europe to the west (as well as Africa), and between Arabia and Egypt to the south and the Euphrates and Mediterranean world to the north, thus increasing commerce and trade throughout the Jewish lands.[42]

The Jews, of course, had long been involved in trading. However, during the period of the Roman empire travel and trade were even more brisk as merchants found more accessible markets for their products.[43] Again we emphasize that the bulk of trading and commercial activities was limited to the native aristocracy of large landowners who, according to Rostovtzeff, were not only "rulers of the land and leaders in its religious life, but capitalists and merchants on a big scale who sometimes added to their wealth by daring speculation."[44]

If we are to believe that James's message is addressed to and has meaning in a Palestinian milieu, then some or all of the merchants referred to in 4:13–17 must be those in Palestine in the first part of the first century A.D. But the question of how much trade and commerce Palestinian Jews were involved in prior to the Jewish War of A.D. 66–70 is not settled. Part of the problem lies in the following statement of Josephus, which is more apologetic than historical:

> Well ours is not a maritime country; neither commerce nor the intercourse which it promotes with the outside world has any attraction for us. Our cities are built inland, remote from the sea; and we devote ourselves to the cultivation of the productive country with which we are blessed.[45]

A number of scholars have pointed out that Josephus's statement has some truth to it, but there is some evidence that Jews did engage in "maritime commerce, owned ships, and even participated in Mediterranean piracy" prior to the Jewish war.[46] Joseph Klausner, for instance, contends that trade and commerce were prevalent.[47] Though Klausner has presented some valuable evidence, he has not demonstrated sufficiently that Jews were involved to a large extent in international trade. At the same time it seems that Josephus is inaccurate in reporting that the Jews were not involved in merchandizing.[48]

In fact, trade and commerce to a large degree were limited to a small segment of the society (that is, the rich merchants to whom James's message is very apropos) and in particular to the Sadducees. Josephus declares that the Sadducees were unable to persuade any but the rich and that the populace was not obsequious to them.[49] However, the Sadducees had great power, and in light of their dominance in the economic life of the country, the prayer of the high priest (who usually belonged to the Sadducean party) on the Day of Atonement is of particular interest: "Our God and God of our fathers, may this year be a year of low prices [because of the hope for an abundant crop[50]], a year of plenty, and a year of *business dealings* [emphasis added]."[51]

That there were years of abundance and years of prosperity for trade for some persons is evident from the data regarding the fertility of Palestine. Both the Talmud and Josephus, as well as Aristeas, paint a picture of Palestine as a very fertile place.[52] All around the countryside of Palestine there was much agricultural production—fruits, grains, vineyards, and olive groves.[53] Of course during the drought years the economy suffered. But this led to increased travel and trade by the Palestinian merchants who had to seek their wealth in other provinces.

Palestinian merchants were not only dependent on agricultural produce for their wealth. Marine life was abundant and large volumes of asphalt were produced in Palestine—the Gospels speak much about the former and Pliny and Strabo about the latter.[54]

Because of the locale of the city of Jerusalem one might conclude that it was poor in trade and commerce, but Joachim Jeremias has documented that despite the city's unfavorable position, it was rich in trade and commerce.[55] Most of the trade, however, involved imports rather than exports. Thus, if Jerusalem is understood as being referred to in James's statement in 4:13 (and it is very possible that Jerusalem should be understood along with other places), it would be "the town" to which the merchants went to spend a year to trade and get gain.

Travelers went to Jerusalem from all over the then known world. Although activated mainly by religious motives, travel was also prompted by political and economic motives.[56] Owners of capital had always been attracted to Jerusalem—wholesalers, tax collectors, and Jews of the Diaspora who had grown rich.[57] The merchant profession was held in great respect in Jerusalem, and even priests engaged in commerce. The high priest's family carried on a flourishing trade in the city,[58] and even the Temple became an important factor in the commerce of Jerusalem.

What we have attempted to demonstrate briefly thus far is that James did not speak in a vacuum when he wrote in 1:11 of the rich man in his businesss pursuits and in 4:13 regarding those who travel to trade and get gain.[59] James's speech is based on the socioeconomic realities of his milieu which had its commercial roots in the Hellenistic times and which could find analogies throughout the Roman world of the first century. But James's cry seems to be particularly directed at the merchants who throughout Syro-Palestine found commercial activity a relatively easy enterprise and a "number one" priority—the accumulation of wealth was their ultimate goal. The description of the availability of raw material and the ease with which the wealthy entrepreneurs could reach their destination and dispose of their goods makes more understandable the arrogant assertion: "Today or tomorrow we will go into such a town and spend a year there and trade and get gain."

James's valuation of these merchants is not only clear in his statements in 1:10-11 and 4:14, but it becomes even more perspicuous when seen in the light of Jewish and non-Jewish literature from which he might have drawn. Besides the famous parable of the rich fool in Luke 12:16-20, one could take note of the polemic which the wisdom teacher Ben Sirach uttered against the unscrupulous speculators in their hectic hunt for riches:

When he says, "I have found rest,
and now I shall enjoy my goods!"
he does not know how much time will pass
until he leaves them to others and dies.[60]

The apocalypse of Enoch also pronounces woes upon those
who "acquire silver and gold in unrighteousness"; their
"riches shall not abide," but shall "speedily ascend" from
them.[61] If there is any dependence by James on these passages,
it is evident that he does not see these merchants of his day as
mere traders doing an honest business, but rather as unscrupulous and unrighteous speculators whose reward is sure.

It is also possible that James, like Seneca, was drawing on
contemporary literature (which in many instances was building on Greek diatribe and was part of popular Greco-Roman
philosophy in general). Most significant is Seneca's 101st Epistle, "On the Futility of Planning Ahead." He begins by stating
that every day and every hour reveal that we are nothing and
that as we plan for eternity our weaknesses compel us to look
over our shoulders at death, which relentlessly pursues us. Of
greatest interest for us is the philosopher's narration of the
Roman knight Cornelius Senecio, who fits almost perfectly
the picture painted by James. Seneca speaks of him as

he who was venturing investments by land and sea, who
had also entered public life and left no type of business
untried, [and who,] during the very realization of financial success and during the very onrush of the money that
flowed into his coffers, was snatched from the world [by
death]![62]

The Roman philosopher, like James, goes on to bemoan the
futility of such living:

How foolish it is to set out one's life, when one is not even
owner of the morrow! O what madness it is to plot our

far-reaching hopes! To say: "I will buy and build, loan and call in money, win titles of honor, and then, old and full of years I will surrender myself to a life of ease." Believe me when I say everything is doubtful, even for those who are prosperous. No one has any right to draw himself upon the future. . . . We plan distant voyages and long-postponed home-comings after roaming over foreign shores . . . and all the while death stands at our side.[63]

James's language regarding such a merchant, however, is much harsher than Seneca's. This of course fits into the former's conception of the rich. For him the rich persons of his time were unrighteous, unscrupulous, oppressive to the poor, and arrogant. Thus with great emphasis he accuses them of boasting in their arrogance[64] an arrogance which "implies confidence in one's cleverness, luck, strength, skill, etc."[65] But all such cleverness and arrogance is of no use, for it is outside of God's will—a will which favors the poor and rejects the arrogance of the rich. The one possessing such a clever and arrogant attitude is like a flower which fades with the scorching heat (1:11) or like a mist which vanishes (4:14).

At 4:17 James ends the passage dealing with the merchants with a maxim which poses a problem to many expositors. For example it is seen as "an isolated aphorism . . . with no real relation to what precedes or to what follows," and it is further suggested that this is probably the reason the RSV drops the connecting particle *oun* ("therefore")—although there is no authority in the Greek manuscripts for this omission. All that can be said, it is claimed, is that the writer inserted the aphorism at random.[66]

We must admit that the maxim does not fit well or logically into the passage. At the same time we cannot ignore the *oun,* which implies that as far as the author is concerned, this maxim is some sort of a concluding statement.[67] The most, however, that can be suggested here regarding its meaning within the context of the pericope is that, as far as James is concerned, the commercial schemers knew better than to act as they did and failed to perform accordingly. Therefore, their actions were sinful.

CHAPTER 6

The Rich Agriculturalists and the Poor: James 5:1–6

With 5:1–6 James concludes his final attack on the rich. From a denunciation of a spirit of arrogant financial scheming, he turns to a spirit even more obnoxious and wicked—a spirit which is selfish, tyrannical, and oppressive[1]—and actions so oppressive that the cries of the oppressed have reached the ears of the "Lord of Host."

Again James cries *age nun,* as in 4:13. The *nun* ("now"), as we mentioned earlier, increased intensity, and the *age* ("go") indicated an insistent, somewhat brusque address.[2] But the repetition of the cry heightens to an even greater degree the author's denunciation of the rich, and his attitude toward them comes to peak in the harsh language of the passage.

The highly rhetorical language is in the style of the Old Testament prophets (and also parallels Jewish apocalyptic as well as echoing the teaching of Jesus). As in the Old Testament the address is not intended to influence the rich. They were no more part of the listening congregation than the nations and peoples addressed in Isaiah 34:1. These fulminations then were not a call to repentance. Rather they were probably intended more as a comfort and consolation to the oppressed who could be solaced by the fact that ultimate judgment would be meted out upon their oppressors.[3]

It should be noted at this point that even if an argument could be successfully mounted to make "rich and poor" in the other parts of James equal to "wicked and righteous," it is clear that in 5:1–6 the context is dealing with literal economic conditions. It is therefore amazing that there are scholars who have postulated the opinion that in 5:1–6 "rich' is symbolic, indicating the spiritual self-delusion of the Jews![4] But we must again point out that the question of whether the audience being addressed is Christian and non-Christian is irrelevant to James here. The author is not working with that motif, but simply with the motif of the economically rich and poor. It is to the economically rich persons who oppress the poor that James offers no call to repentance, but only pronouncements of judgment.

Probably one of the main reasons James has no words of repentance for the rich is that they are viewed by him as an ungodly social caste (as indicated by the vocative with the article *hoi plousioi* ["the rich"].[5] There is no hope for any rich persons as long as they are members of that class; there is only judgment and damnation. They are told to weep and "howl" *(ololuzontes).* In the New Testament the latter verb is found only here in James 5:1, but it is found in the LXX. In the oracle against Babylon in Isaiah 13:6 the prophet calls upon the empire to "wail, for the day of the Lord is near, as destruction from the Almighty it will come." And in 13:8 the ancient prophet states that "pangs of anguish will seize them; they will be in anguish like a woman in travail" (see also Isa. 14:31; 15:3). It is quite possible that these passages were in the mind of James, and if this is so, then this "onomatopoetic word *[ololuzontes]* vividly describes the howls of rage and pain of the damned,"[6] as it did in the Isaiah denunciation.

James presents the rich as commiting two main crimes: (1) luxurious living, and (2) oppression.[7] The first is explicated initially in vv. 2–3, which speak of the luxurious articles of wealth which have been hoarded. When writing these verses

James might have been thinking of the Testament of Issachar, which speaks of the single-minded person who "coveteth not gold, he overreacheth not his neighbor, he longeth not after manifold dainties, he delighteth not in varied apparel."[8]

However, the verses in James call to mind even more the teachings of Jesus in Matthew 6:19 regarding the laying up of treasure on earth "where moth and rust consume." There are, however, those who contend that the apparent relation of James 5:2–3 to Matthew 6:19 is superficial. It is noted that quite different Greek words are used for "rust" (and the Matthean *brōsis* may not mean "rust" but "worms"). Furthermore it is claimed that while Matthew 6:19 is not addressed to 'rich" persons but persons with moderate means, James addressed the truly rich.[9] We do not, however, believe that the relation is necessarily superficial. James could certainly have been employing the same textual tradition as Matthew and simply decided that it was appropriate for and could be adopted by an audience of a different class than that addressed by Matthew. (The question can be raised as to whether the members of Jesus' audience were actually laying up treasures, or whether he was warning them against such. To suggest that Jesus was addressing persons of moderate means is a hypothesis that might be hard to substantiate.) What James would actually be borrowing is the general motif and, therefore, to have the exact words is not essential.

Even if those traditions and sayings were at the back of the author's mind, it seems more than likely that in the forefront of his thinking was the actual situation around him. The possession of much clothing (as in the case of one Lucullus who claimed to have five thousand cloaks at home[10]) was a customary sign of wealth, and the hoarding of clothing was popular.[11] As a matter of fact it has been noted that it is still the Oriental fashion to heap up garments, shawls, carpets, and all manner of goods as the stuff of a princely home.[12]

For James all these signs of wealth are worthless, and he uses the perfect tense to emphasize the point. The question here, however, is how we shall understand the use of the perfect tense. If we interpret it logically, it gives the impression that the disaster has already come upon the rich, but there is yet more to come. Some expositors tend to such an interpretation and point out that for James the last days had already begun, and with them all earthly values had lost their meaning.[13] Others, however, feel that a logical interpretation contradicts the mood of the pericope, and, therefore, interpret the verb as prophetic perfects—they express "the prophetic anticipation of things to come, and therefore a future meaning results: Your wealth will be of no more use to you at that time, for it will be gone."[14] We concur with this latter interpretation, for the motif of the new age having already begun is not found in James; rather the language of James seems to indicate that judgment is still in the future, and the prosperity of the rich is still very much evident.[15] But those riches will one day be evidence against them and will be part of the judgment on them.[16]

With v. 4 James takes up the cause of the poor, oppressed, and exploited agricultural laborers[17]—a class which "from ancient times down to the migratory workers and sharecroppers of the modern American era . . . [has] been among the most exploited of peoples."[18] It is as if the oppression of that class were the ultimate crime the rich could commit. So grievious is their fraudulent treatment of the laborers that James states that the cries of the oppressed have reached the ears of the Lord of Host *(Sabaōth)*. This title seems to combine "majesty and transcendence and emphasizes that the cause of the poor is to come before the supreme Sovereign, whose justice is now to be visited upon the rich."[19] C. Leslie Mitton has beautifully described how the use of that name for God illustrates God's concern for the poor:

It is the same God, who created the sun, moon and stars, and who orders their courses, who is also deeply concerned about the just treatment of the poor and insignificant, ready to defend them from injustice and punish the wrongdoers. As in Ps. 147:3–4, the One who heals the broken-hearted is the same mighty God who "determined the number of the stars," so here (and also at Isa. 5:9) He who is Lord of Host is the protector of the oppressed and ill-treated.[20]

James's injunction in v. 4 against withholding the wages of laborers goes back in Judaism to the Mosaic laws. In Leviticus 19:13 we find the regulation: "The wages of a hired servant shall not remain with you all night until morning" (see also Deut. 24:14–15; Mal. 3:5). Rabbinic literature also affirms these instructions:

> Whoever withholds the wages of a hired laborer transgresses these five prohibitions of five denominations and one affirmative precept as follows: Thou shalt not oppress thy neighbour; neither rob him; thou shalt not oppress an hired servant that is poor. The wages of him that is hired shall not abide all night with thee; at his day shalt thou give him his hire; and neither shall the sun go down upon it.[21]

The intertestamental literature also quotes the Levitical text, as seen in Tobit 4:14. But like James, Ben Sirach goes further than the Mosaic precept and suggests that the refusal to pay laborers was murder:

> To take away a neighbor's living is to murder him:
> To deprive an employee of his wages is to shed blood.[22]

Verse 4 in James makes it very clear that the oppressive rich were the big landowners. This is evident from the word *chōras,* which designates large farms or tracts of lands[23]—a whole estate under one ownership.[24] It was against these plutocrats that our author's indignation was aroused.

It should be noted that the problem of large landowners dominating the economic scene of the first century was a matter of concern to more than just the biblical writers. Seneca, the Roman writer who lived from 4 B.C. to A.D. 65, denounced avarice and human craving for overmuch as the cause of poverty—a craving which brought an end to the happy age of communal existence. He then goes on to show how this *avaritia* brought oppression to the poor and added estate to estate of the big landowner: "She adds one estate to another, evicting a neighbor either by buying him out or by wronging him. . . . She extends her country-seats to the size of provinces and defines ownership as meaning extensive travel through one's own property."[25]

This state of affairs was not limited to Italy, but in other places thousands of farmers were tilling and digging to fill *one* "single belly."[26] Empire-wide there was an increasing concentration of rural wealth in the hands of just a few. Numerous cruel pressures were exerted by the strong landowners against the weak, by "the arrogant rich, 'the powerful,' against the adjoining farm, villagers, or 'the poor,' sometimes by crooked litigation, sometimes by armed force."[27]

This concentration of landownership in a few hands was also part of Palestinian economic life. As a matter of fact, as far back as the eighth century B.C. the prophet Isaiah spoke of those who despoiled the poor by adding "field to field":

Woe to those who join house to house,
Who add field to field,
until there is no more room,
and you are made to dwell alone
in the midst of the land [Isa. 5:8; see 3:14–15].

This oppressive situation led to "grave economic problems and acute distress of the country population."[28]

By the first century A.D. this situation had become even more acute. More and more estates, which were generally worked by slaves, serfs, tenants, and hired laborers, were consolidated into the hands of those few with vast holdings.[29] The rich became richer by adding estate to estate through the confiscation of the property of not only the small landowners but also of those nobility who fell out of grace with the ruler, for instance Herod the Great.[30]

Absenteeism was a further aspect of the exploitation by these big landowners.[31] Many of those who owned property in the country were the wealthy of the city, particularly Jerusalem. Interestingly, the tenants, serfs, and day laborers did not always take the exploitation by the absentee landlord passively. The Zenon papyri mention goods being withheld from an absentee landowner and the collector being driven off.[32]

The oppression by the landowners also functioned through the judicial system. The Mishnah notes that cases concerning property were decided by three judges.[33] However, in many instances the bench was ursurped by a single big property owner who had the "reputation for oppressive and venal verdicts."[34]

In first-century Palestine the aristocracy of landowners was made up of both leaders in religious life and rulers of the land. They were the capitalists, the big proprietors, the large merchants, and "the major party of the propertied class in Israel."[35] These were the Sadducees (although according to Josephus some Pharisees were also landowners[36]). Around them a "small knot of moneyed owners and rackrenters" rallied.[37] The Sadducees formed an aristocracy not only of wealth but of landownership.[38] When Josephus states that they were not able to persuade any but the rich and had no following among the populace,[39] he is elucidating a profound tension betwen the Sadducees and the poor.

James's diatribe against the rich landowners and his conception of them are definitely contrary to the opinion of Rabbi Eleazar, who argues that engaging in business is more profitable than working as a farmer.[40] Heinz Kreissig has shown that the life of the landlord in Palestine was very profitable.[41] In first-century Palestine the division of work between landlord and merchant was not as developed as in later centuries. Both commerce and farming were directly linked. The landlords or their agents brought their goods to the market and dominated the market.[42] The tenant who had to compete with such a landlord appeared beside him as a mere small vendor.[43] On the one hand, the landlord had the better produce to market, and this assured his dominance of the market.[44] The big landowner produced better products, for he had larger holdings and controlled the fertile lowlands.[45] On the other hand, the small farmer had to eke out a living from a small plot of land which was generally in the stony and unproductive hill country.[46] Ben Sira recognized this sorry situation when he said of such a poor farmer: "On the height of mountains is his vineyard and the earth of his vineyard is washed down into the vineyards of others."[47]

With this type of situation it is obvious that even in normal times when the big Palestinian farmer was reaping a fivefold harvest (and up to a hundredfold in excellent seasons), the small farmer could not compete with his wealthier counterpart, for his land could not produce the quality products which would make them competitive. The small farmer normally had no choice then but to become a wage earner, the big landlord being his master; this is the kind of situation to which James is making reference.

It should also be noted that even if small farmers had fertile land there were other problems that had to be faced which would push them out of business. For example, it was difficult to get proper tools. Tools such as hoes, spades, and iron plowshares were not made by the farmer's family as they once had been; special manual workers such as the blacksmith and potter arose and took on that role. However, for the small farmer to purchase tools (and also the beast of burden, such as the donkey, which would assist in the threshing), he would need a surplus of produce for exchange. But such a surplus he did not have. And even if he was able to sell his small and inferior products against the competition of others, the funds gained would probably be too small to purchase the tools necessary for better production.[48]

The small farmer was also pushed out of business and into the category of a wage earner by the crookedness of the big landlord at the marketplace. In the years of abundance the large landowner had such large quantities of goods that he could undersell the small farmer who could not compete with such low prices, especially in light of the quality of his products.[49] It was therefore just about impossible for him to make enough of a profit to live on. The situation was even more disastrous during years of drought. In the bad years the wealthy property owner could hoard his goods and thus inflate the prices. Then the small farmer was almost totally at the mercy of the manipulative landlords who controlled the marketplace.[50]

The difficulties encountered by the small holder vis-à-vis the large landowner were not limited to the manipulations of the big proprietor in the marketplace. The giving of loans, the pressure exercised in the collection of loans, and the very real threat of expropriation on account of nonpayment of loans were a great source of tension.[51]

How extremely critical the situation was in the repayment of loans is evident in the promulgation of the prosbul by Hillel toward the end of the first century B.C. This legal formula allowed a creditor to collect a debt even during the Sabbatical Year, even though Moses gave an injunction against it (Deut. 15:2). The formula states: "I affirm to you, such-a-one and such-a-one, the judges in such-a-place, that, touching any debt due to me, I will collect it whensoever I will."[52] The Mishnah further states that it was when Hillel saw that the people refrained from giving loans that he instituted the prosbul.[53] It is possible that this halakhic ordinance was for the advantage of the rich as well as the poor, as the Talmud suggests.[54] However, no matter what its original intention was, this grave modification of a fundamental Mosaic law must have overall been more to the disadvantage of the poor, as is evident from the fact that at the outbreak of the Jewish revolt in A.D. 66 one of the first acts of the Zealots was to "burn the contracts belonging to their creditors, and thereby dissolve their obligation for paying their debts."[55]

We have shown thus far that the pitiful condition of the small holder was brought on by a number of factors. The confiscation of property by powerful political figures, like Herod, reduced the small owners to the state of tenants or hirelings. The dominance of the marketplace by the big proprietor through economic manipulation both in normal and poor years resulted in the small farmer not being able to make enough profit to take care of his basic household needs, much less a surplus to procure the necessary work implements for the farm. This would of necessity drive him to give up his farm and become a laborer for the big landowner. In many instances the option left open to these small holders was to obtain a loan from their wealthier neighbors. Repayment by the debtor was very difficult and the pressure exerted by the creditor for that repayment resulted in many small holdings being expropriated. The debt-ridden owner was forced either to sell himself into slavery to the rich landowner or to sink to the level of a day laborer.[56]

Those day laborers were the mowers and harvesters with whom James was sympathetic because of the oppression brought upon them by their employers. Such oppression was condemned in the law codes of Deuteronomy:

> You shall not oppress a hired servant who is poor and needy, whether he is one of your brethren or one of the sojourners who are in your land within your towns; you shall give him his hire on the day he earns it before the sun goes down (for he is poor, and sets his heart upon it); lest he cry against you to the Lord, and it be sin in you [Deut. 24:14–15].[57]

Rabbinic law also enjoined the prompt payment of wages.[58] As a matter of fact, it has been noted that an employer used to enter into an agreement with a worker, usually by word of mouth, and whoever broke the contract would be fined, whether employee or employer. Joseph Klausner has further commented that "the sympathy shown in the *Mishna* and *Tosefta* in favor of the laborer redounds to the Talmud's credit." However, he suggests that this sympathy was "mainly no more than an academic view never widely held in real life."[59] That this must be true is made clear by James's concern.

The sorry state of the situation of the laborers was even more aggravated by the fact that the avenues of protest available to many dissatisfied workers today were denied their ancient prototypes. For example, we find a paucity of strikes throughout the entire Greco-Roman world, and they are almost entirely absent in Palestine. This was partially (if not mainly) due to the existence of slavery.[60] Because of the large army of slaves (as well as the numerous unemployed), strikes as a form of redress were futile.[61] Society was not based on the work of the hired laborer but upon the slave. Kautsky has clearly noted:

> Today all society is based on the labor of the proletarian. . . . Society did not live off the proletariat then; the proletariat lived off society. It was quite superfluous and could have disappeared altogether without hurting society; it would have done it good instead. The labor of slaves was the foundation on which society was based.[62]

Even though this was more true in the Greco-Roman world outside Palestine than in Palestine itself, the fact that there were slaves, as well as a great unemployed "reserve army," made it very easy for the large landowners to keep down (or hold back) the wages and depress the economic level of the free laborer.[63] With this intolerable situation and with laborers at the mercy of the wealthy agricultural bosses, the only viable avenue of protest left open for some of the farmers was to cry unto the Lord—as is mentioned in James.

The economic pressures, however, led others to seek other avenues of redress. Many turned to brigandage and highway robbery. Many were imbued with a spirit of violent rage and revolt and involved themselves in revolutionary movements of the Zealots and Sicarii. These movements (it is generally accepted) were involved not only in civil and social revolt against Rome but also in social and economic revolt against the local, ruling rich class that they saw as their political, social, economic, and national enemy. Josephus reports regarding their violent activities:

> The impostors and brigands, banding together, incited numbers to revolt, exhorting them to assert their independence, and threatening to kill any who submitted to Roman domination and forcibly to suppress those who voluntarily accepted servitude. Distributing themselves in companies throughout the country, they *looted the houses of the wealthy, murdered their owners,* and set the villages on fire [emphasis added].[64]

Interestingly, Ralph Martin has argued for a *Sitz im Leben* of James which grows out of a concern for the methods of redress adopted by these revolutionaries. Martin actually argues for a "setting" of the epistle in which James opposes injustice and defends the poor (particularly the poor priests) against the Sadducean aristocracy and Agrippa I, who tried to suppress the poor. However, he points out that there is another side to the author's teaching: he deplores the violence, anger, and killing acted out by the Zealots and Sicarii (to whom the poor and oppressed had turned) and counseled against impatient actions.[65] Whether or not Martin's theory has merit the fact remains that economic pressures felt by the laborers led many to violent actions. At the same time it is evident that many sought release by crying to God and turning hopefully to spiritual messianic movements.

The emphasis of James, however (and this is further evident in vv. 4–6), is on the cruelty of the rich; he accuses them of murder—an accusation made about two centuries earlier by Ben Sirach:

> The bread of the needy is the life of the poor;
> whoever deprives them of it is a man of blood.
> To take away a neighbor's living is to murder him;
> to deprive an employee of his wages is to shed blood.[66]

It is possible that in James "murder" is not used in the bodily sense, but rather refers to the economic oppression of the poor by the rich.[67] Rabbinic literature attests also to such an understanding of murder, but with even more physical overtones.[68] But it seems clear to us that James has not only economic tyranny in mind but physical violence as well. In line with this it is interesting to read the following comments by Tom Hanks:

> It is fascinating, though profoundly disturbing, to see the conservative evangelical mentality at work to make James more palatable. In James 4, in a description of class struggle ("wars," "fights," "ye fight," "ye war," verses 1–2) motivated by greed ("ye covet," verse 2), and expressing itself in all manner of capitalist initiatives ("we will trade and we will make a profit," verse 13), James says directly "you murder" (verse 2b). "Murder?" say the commentators. "Impossible, free enterprise, capitalist ingenuity, the American way of life, an honest buck; what's good for General Motors is good for the country." But James says "you murder." The mechanisms of oppression deprive the poor of their land and other means of livelihood and leave them without the essentials for life (1 Kings 21; Luke 16:19–31).[69]

Apart from his concluding accusation of murder, James ends the pericope with a very significant point: *ouk antitassetai humin.* This phrase is frequently taken to indicate the passiveness of helpless laborers who can not or will not resist their brutal oppressors.[70] In a brief note, however, Luis Alonso Schökel has taken this translation and interpretation to task. He argues that for one to correctly interpret this passage, a stylistic device in 4:6 must be recognized. This device he calls "thematic announcement" and says it "consists of a sentence in which the author announced the subject(s) to be developed."[71] The theme having been developed, 5:6 resumes the statement of 4:6 and uses it as the conclusion of the commentary. This proposition solves a number of difficulties with 5:6: first, it explains the violent change from aorist to present tense,[72] and, second, it solves the problem of a lack of an explicit subject (as well as making understandable the seeming abrupt beginning of the sentence without a syntactical link) by making the subject, as in 4:6, *ho theos* ("God").[73] The line of development between the inclusio (4:6–5:6) is, therefore: "God opposes the arrogant, you behave arrogantly, should not He oppose you?"[74]

This interpretation fits very well the strong social justice stance of James, especially in this latter pericope (5:1–6). To read the concluding remark as a statement of passivism is wholly out of character with the denunciatory nature of James's final diatribe against the rich.[75] As a matter of fact, stylistically the passivist reading does not fit the schema of the passage—a schema which emphasizes the judgment on the rich. A quick glance at Schökel's schematization illustrates this:

(a) you do such and such . . . for the last day (1–3)
(b) the man you have wronged appeals to the Judge against you (4)
(c) you do such and such . . . for the day of slaughter (5)
(d) you do such and such . . . Should not He oppose you? (6).[76]

It must be noted, however, that simply because this interpretation rejects the passivist reading of the verse, it does not necessarily follow that James supports violent revolutionary expressions by the oppressed. As a matter of fact, v. 6 unequivocally makes such actions God's prerogative. Besides, v. 7 clearly spells out the role of the poor in relation to the rich: they must be patient, seeing that judgment is in the hand of God.

Because of the intense apocalyptic nature of James's cry for judgment on the rich, it is important to try to determine the thought-world out of which he speaks. Is he speaking from a Christian eschatological perspective or is his language about a Day of Judgment adapted from Jewish apocalypticism?

It is widely held that James, along with the earliest Christians, believed in the imminence of the Parousia of Christ, at which time Christ would bring judgment upon the wicked. It is suggested by some scholars that James does not demand any social justice for the victims of the rich oppressors because he believes the End is near and assumes that his days are the last days: "The whole order of things was to be swept away immediately, and the thought of any reform and redress on earth never entered the mind of James."[77] It is assumed that James's thinking is similar to that of Paul, who instigated no social reform, but rather admonished each person to remain in the state in which he or she was called, because of the imminence of the Parousia (see 1 Cor 7:20–24, 26).[78]

However, the language of James, especially in 5:1–6, is quite different from that of Paul. It is so different that it is suggested that "we are in the presence of a manner of archaic speaking previous to the period where the Pauline prediction had imposed on the word Parousia the technical sense which it subsequently preserved."[79] This "maniere de parler archaique" is the Day of Judgment motif of the classical prophets as well as the apocalyptic literature of Judaism. The description in James 5:1, where the author invites the rich to weep and howl for the miseries which are coming upon them, recalls the announcements by the prophets of the catastrophies which would come upon the wicked. An example of the announcments is the *Dies Irae* of Zephaniah:

> Wail, O inhabitants of the Mortar!
> For all the traders are no more;
> all who weigh out silver are cut off. . . .
> Their goods shall be plundered,
> and their houses laid waste. . . .
> The sound of the day of the Lord is bitter,
> the mighty man cries aloud there.
> A day of wrath is that day,
> a day of distress and anguish [Zeph. 1:11–15].

But even more significant is the judgment upon the rich being called "a day of slaughter." This manner of speaking recalls the prophetic prediction of carnage and war and slaughter which would be inflicted upon the nations or Jerusalem.[80]

The apocalyptic threat of judgment upon the rich in James recalls even more strikingly the intertestamental apocalyptic ideas. One cannot fail to observe the striking resemblance in language and thought between James and Ethiopian Enoch. To illustrate we look at a section of Enoch's "woes" upon the rich oppressors:

> Woe to those who build unrighteousness and oppres-
>   sion . . .
> For they shall be suddenly overthrown, . . .
> And by the sword shall they fall.
> And those who acquire gold and silver in judgement
>   suddenly shall perish. . . .
> Woe to you, ye rich, for ye have trusted in your riches,
> And from your riches shall ye depart. . . .
> [Ye] have become ready for *the day of slaughter,*
> And the day of darkness and the day of great judge-
>   ment. . . .

And for your fall there shall be no compassion,
and your Creator will rejoice at your destruction. . . .
Woe to them who work unrighteousness and help oppression,
and slay their neighbours until the day of the great
judgement.[81]

The conclusion which we believe can be extricated from this comparison between James and the apocalyptic writers and prophets is that James's denunciation corresponds to the ancient conception of the judgment—a judgment on the rich which was far more violent than that found anywhere else in the New Testament (with the possible exception of Rev. 18). But it is a judgment which brings hope and satisfaction to the poor. God's judgment brings about the Great Reversal—the powerful rich and oppressive exploiters are given over to damnation, and the oppressed who have waited patiently receive the eternal reward.

Finally, it is necessary to emphasize that although James's strong fulminations against the oppressive rich of his day are apocalyptic and point ultimately to the Final Judgment, his message was relevant to his age and is relevant to ours. His words speak not only of the other world, but address this world. His intense language demonstrates that he opposes the structures that enable the rich to increase their wealth at the expense of the poor—structures that fatten some and allow them to live in luxury while others are exploited and live in misery and filth, eking out a mere existence. James's indignation is an unqualified condemnation of the intolerable nature of such an existence. His epistle condemns unjust situations in his and our historical contexts.

The principal purpose of James's attack upon the rich is to give consolation and comfort to the poor and oppressed, and yet that attack also harbors a strong social justice stance. It is true that James does not suggest that the poor should violently overthrow the rich in order to obtain justice. James is quite clear that *God* is one who will accomplish the violent overthrow of the rich because of their unjust exploitation of the poor. Judgment, overthrow, and slaughter are in the hands of the Lord. However, it is also true that James states that God hears the cry of the poor. God responds to the cry and struggle of the poor. Thus the oppressed have the right to cry out to God to demand their just due. That God is attentive to the cry of the poor demonstrates that they have every right to demand a just wage and that which is owed them, that is, justice and the rewards of their labor.

Because James's harsh and intense language in 1:27, in 2:1–26, and in 5:1–6 manifests his strong social justice stance toward issues in his (and our) context, it is clear that James equates true religion with social concern and that for him one's personal religion is not all that counts in the final reckoning. As in Matthew 25:31–46, James reveals that one's social involvement in the present is as important as one's personal religious practices and that, in fact, personal religion is meaningless without social commitment. This in essence is the profound meaning of James's statement that "faith by itself, if it has no works, is dead" (2:17).

Throughout much of the scriptures, God's option for the poor is explicit. It is forcefully revealed when in James 5:1–6 God is shown to be attentive to the cry of the oppressed. That James takes up their cause as an apostle of Jesus Christ demonstrates his option for the poor. Like James, we, as modern representatives of Jesus Christ, are called to take that option and to take up the cause of the oppressed.

Notes

INTRODUCTION

1. We must note, however, that New Testament sociologists do utilize Form and Redaction Criticism in their study of the New Testament documents. Besides, Dietfried Gewalt, "Neutestamentliche Exegese und Soziologie," *Evangelische Theologie* 31 (1971): 88–99, and Klaus Berger, *Exegese des Neuen Testaments* (Heidelberg: Quelle and Meyer, 1977), p. 219, among others, have argued that Form Criticism opens the way for a sociological interpretation, or at least for asking social questions in their concern for the *Sitz im Leben* of the pericope; see Robin Scroggs, "The Sociological Interpretation of the New Testament: The Present State of Research," *New Testament Studies* 26 (1980): 165 n.2. Wayne Meeks, however, has rightly pointed out that the sociological component which was so important in Hermann Gunkel's pioneer research in Form Criticism has largely been forgotten in Form and Redaction Criticism ("The Social World of Early Christianity," *The Council on the Study of Religion Bulletin* 6 [1975]: 5); cf. Leander E. Keck, "On the Ethos of Early Christians," *Journal of the American Academy of Religion* 42 (1974): 446–50; Jonathan Z. Smith, "The Social Description of Early Christianity," *Religious Studies Review* 1 (1975): 19; John G. Gager, *Kingdom and Community: The Social World of Early Christianity* (Englewood Cliffs, N.J.: Prentice-Hall, 1975), p. 10.

2. John K. Riches in a paper presented at the 1983 Society of Biblical Literature meetings contends that there should be no sharp divide between theology and the sociology of the New Testament. A full understanding of the author's or the community's belief will involve an exploration of their social context—their social attitudes and patterns of behavior ("The Sociology of Matthew: Some Basic Questions Concerning Its Relation to the Theology of the New Testament," in *Society of Biblical Literature 1983 Seminar Papers* [Chico, Calif.: Scholars Press, 1983], pp. 259–71, esp. 264–68). Early in the paper Riches notes that "in the past there has been a tendency on the part of Biblical scholars to think that what was required in order to discover the sense of a particular passage was a full and sure grasp of the particular language in which it was written. Clearly this is important, but equally it is not sufficient" (p. 261).

3. Abraham Malherbe, *Social Aspects of Early Christianity* (Baton Rouge: Louisana State University Press, 1977), p. 17. See also pp. 15–20 passim.

4. Robin Scroggs, however, has cautioned that "most texts are speaking about theological verities, not sociological conditions. The sociologist must read the text as if it were palimpsest. This means the researcher must work with the utmost caution and strictness with adequate guard against over-enthusiasm" (p. 166). But Scroggs should recognize that in many instances one cannot separate the theological verities

from the sociological conditions to which these truths are addressed.

5. It can be noted here that Old Testament scholarship has utilized sociological theories as a method since the nineteenth century. An example of this is seen in a work by S. T. Kimbrough, Jr., that discusses and analyzes Antonin Causse's (the nineteenth- and twentieth-century French sociologist) sociological method. Kimbrough points out that Causse was the "first competent Old Testament scholar to present a broad synthesis of Israel's social evolution drawing upon Durkheim, Lévy-Bruhl, Pedersin, Weber, and Frazer" *(Israelite Religion in Sociological Perspective: The Work of Antonin Causse* [Wiesbaden: Otto Harrassowitz, 1978], p. 125). Cf. Norman K. Gottwald's article "Sociological Method in the Study of Ancient Israel," in *The Bible and Liberation: Political and Social Hermeneutics,* ed. Norman K. Gottwald (Maryknoll, N.Y.: Orbis, 1983), pp. 26–37; and his mammoth work *The Tribes of Yahweh: A Sociology of the Religion of Liberated Israel, 1250–1050 B.C.E.* (Orbis, 1979).

6. For one of the most recent comprehensive articles, see Bruce J. Malina, 'The Social Sciences and Biblical Interpretation," *Interpretation* 37 (1982): 229–42. Cf. John G. Gager, "Shall We Marry Our Enemies," *Interpretation* 37 (1982): 256–65, and his book *Kingdom and Community.* See also Gerd Theissen's numerous essays and works, examples of which are: "Die soziologische Auswertung religiöser Über-lieferungen: Ihre methodologischen Probleme am Beispiel des Urchristentums," *Kairos* 17 (1975): 284–99; "Theoretische Probleme religionssoziologischer Forschung und die Analyse des Urchristentums," *Neue Zeitschrift für systematische Theologie und Religions-philosophie* 16 (1974): 35–56; and *The Social Setting of Pauline Christiantiy* (Philadelphia: Fortress, 1982), esp. chap. 5, "The Sociological Interpretation of Religious Traditions: Its Methodological Problems as Exemplified in Early Christianity." See also the collection of articles under the subheading "Sociological Readings of the New Testament," in *The Bible and Liberation,* ed. Norman Gottwald (Maryknoll, N.Y.: Orbis, 1983), pp. 337–457.

7. Paul W. Hollenbach in his essay "Recent Historical Jesus Studies and the Social Sciences," *Society of Biblical Literature 1983 Seminar Papers* (Chico, Calif.: Scholars Press, 1983, pp. 61–73) has mentioned some of these studies, which include Fernando Belo, *A Materialist Reading of the Gospel of Mark* (Maryknoll N.Y.: Orbis, 1981); John Elliott, *A Home for the Homeless* (Fortress, 1981); H. C. Kee, *Community of the New Age* (Philadelphia: Westminster, 1977); idem, *Christian Origins in Sociological Perspective* (Westminster, 1980); and Wayne A. Meeks, *The First Urban Christians* (New Haven: Yale University Press, 1983), among others mentioned in my notes above. Some others Hollenbach has not noted are: James Alan Wilde, "A Social Description of the Community Reflected in the Gospel of Mark" (Ph.D. dissertation, Drew University, 1974); Alfred Schreiber, *Die Gemeinde in Korinth: Versuch einer gruppendynamischen Bertrachtung der Entwicklung der Gemeinde von Korinth auf der Basis des erseten Korintherbriefs* (Münster: Aschen-dorff, 1977). A number of worthwhile articles (in addition to some mentioned earlier) include Bruce J. Malina, "Limited Good and the Social World of Early Christianity," *Biblical Theology Bulletin* 8 (1978): 162–76; and Sheldon R. Isenberg, "Some Uses and Limitations of Social Scientific Methodology in the Study of Early Christianity," *Society of Biblical Literature 1980 Seminar Papers* (Chico, Calif.: Scholars Press, 1980), pp. 29–49.

8. See Daniel J. Harrington, "Sociological Concepts and the Early Church, a Decade of Research," *Theological Studies* 41 (1980): 183, for his discussion of a number of obstacles to using the technique. We take cognizance of these points, among others.

9. See Byran R. Wilson, *Magic and Millennium: A Sociological Study of*

Religious Movements among Tribal and Third-World Peoples (London: Heinemann, 1973); *Religion in Secular Society: A Sociological Comment* (London: C.A. Watts, 1966); *Sects and Society: A Sociological Study of the Elim Tabernacle, Christian Science and Christadelphians* (Berkeley: University of California Press, 1961); *Religious Sects: A Sociological Study* (New York: McGraw-Hill, 1970).

10. At one of the seminars of the Consultation on Sociology and the New Testament at the 1983 Society of Biblical Literature meetings, a participant suggested that Julian Pitt-Rivers demonstrated in the book *The Fate of Shechem or the Politics of Sex: Essays in Medieval Anthropology* (Cambridge, Eng.: Cambridge University Press, 1977) that it is possible to use modern models to interpret ancient communities.

11. Scroggs, p. 167; cf. L. S. Countryman, *The Rich Christian in the Church of the Early Empire: Contradictions and Accommodations* (New York: Edwin Mellen, 1980), p. 212, who, though welcoming the influence of modern social theory, senses the temptation "to apply such models cross-culturally with no further ado"—especially when dealing with ancient institutions. Interestingly, David Bartlett in his review of Gager's book notes that there is a "need to articulate those methodological steps by which one can move from sociological studies in one place and time to observations about communities in another place and time" ("John G. Gager's *Kingdom and Community:* A Summary and Response," *Zygon* 13 [1978]: 122). See Bruce Malina, "The Social Sciences," pp. 229–30, in which such a methodological attempt is made inadequately.

12. Gerd Theissen, *Sociology of Early Palestinian Christianity* (Philadelphia: Fortress, 1977), p. 28; see Mitchell Reddish, "Review of *Sociology of Early Palestinian Christianity* by Gerd Theissen," *Review and Expositor* 76 (1979): 583.

13. Harrington, p. 183, and cf. p. 188; see also Scroggs, p. 166.

14. See Gager, "Shall We Marry Our Enemies," pp. 264-65; Malina, "The Social Sciences," p. 229; see Malina, "Limited Good," p. 165, for three positive values of using sociological and anthropological models: "(1) it is conducive to better exegesis in that it provides clearer understanding of the meaning of a text in the culture that generated it; (2) it has practical usefulness as a guide in determining the validity of subsequent theology if that theology claims to derive from the Jesus movement as witnessed in the texts; (3) it can be of eminent value in determining the parameters of cross cultural translation and fidelity to a given normative tradition."

15. John H. Elliott, *A Home for the Homeless: A Sociological Exegesis of 1 Peter, Its Situation and Strategy* (Philadelphia: Fortress, 1981), is an exception. Elliott attempts to incorporate all features in his analysis of Peter's epistle.

16. This problem is highlighted by Bartlett, "John G. Gager's *Kingdom and Community,*" when he notes that "Gager has to go to the literary sources, and there he discovers . . . indications of an ethic of poverty, some hints that many Christians were not well-to-do. . . ." Thus, "the model becomes less important than the data" (p. 121). We could have known the data from the sources without recourse to the model.

17. The fact is, as James Wilde notes, "whether one's focus is social facts, social history, social organization, or social world, the overall exegetical enterprise can only be enhanced by social inquiry" ("The Social World of Mark's Gospel: A Word about Method," in *Society of Biblical Literature 1978 Seminar Papers* [Missoula, Mont.: Scholars Press, 1979], p. 67).

18. Donald Guthrie, *New Testament Introduction* (Downers Grove, Ill.: Inter-Varsity, 1973), pp. 740-47.

19. Malcolm Sidebottom notes that the document "shows no sympathy at all with the yearnings of the Graeco-Roman world" (*James, Jude and 2 Peter,* The Century

Bible [Greenwood, S.C.: Attic, 1967], p. 21); see also David Bartlett, "The Epistle of James as a Jewish-Christian Document," *Society of Biblical Literature 1979 Seminar Papers* (Missoula, Mont.: Scholars Press, 1979), 2:173–79); and Edwin A. Judge, "The Early Christians as a Scholastic Community, *"Journal of Religious History* 1 (1960–61): 14, who states that James reflects the legalistic outlook of the Nazarenes; cf. John B. Polhill, "The Life-Situation of the Book of James," *Review and Expositor* 66 (1969): 373–74, for arguments against a Jewish source for James.

20. Sidebottom has shown (p. 8) that the references to Matthew noted in the margins of Nestle's Greek Testament amount to thirty-eight, a quarter of all references to all books of the Bible and Apocrypha; see Adolf Schlatter, *The Church in the New Testament Period* (London: S.P.C.K., 1955), pp. 199–200, for discussion of parallels; cf. Guthrie, p. 743, for a list. Of course John A. T. Robinson is probably correct in arguing that no case can be put forward for the literary dependence of the epistle on the Gospel (*Redating the New Testament* [Philadelphia: Westminster, 1976], p. 125). However, Massey H. Shepherd in "The Epistle of James and the Gospel of Matthew," *Journal of Biblical Literature* 75 (1956): 41–51, places the epistle in the latter part of the first century or the early part of the second century and thus suggests literary dependence—James having been composed in Syria where "Matthew alone was accepted as the Gospel" (p. 49). There is, however, not much proof for Shepherd's contention. Note, however, Polhill who argues that James did not develop out of a Synoptic stream; he suggests that James's form of the sayings of Jesus is more illustrative of that found in the Didache (p. 372). Even though we disagree with Polhill's dating of the Epistle, he may be correct in his suggestion that the only direct literary source which James borrowed from is the Greek Old Testament.

21. See Robinson, pp. 131–33; Guthrie, pp. 747–53, presents six; however, the following three seem minor: (1) the author does not claim to be Jesus' brother; (2) the author makes no reference to the great events of Jesus' life; (3) the author's relation to the other New Testament books is said to be unfavorable to James, Jesus' brother.

22. Savas C. Agourides, "The Origin of the Epistle of St. James: Suggestions for a Fresh Approach," *Greek Orthodox Theological Review* 9 (1963–64): 67–72, tries to solve this by arguing for an Aramaic original which was later translated into Greek.

23. Peter H. Davids in his recent commentary, *The Epistle of James: A Commentary On the Greek Text,* The New International Greek Testament Commentary (Grand Rapids: Eerdmans, 1982), p. 13, suggests a possible two-stage development. He notes that James could have been the author of the first set of homilies or could have had a hand in both stages. Then an amanuensis who was fluent in literary Greek might have assisted James in writing the present product, which could have been redacted during the period A.D. 55–66 or possibly A.D. 75–85 (see p. 22).

24. Josephus, *Antiquities* 20.9.1 (trans. Feldman, LCL); cf. Eusebius, *Church History* 2.23.18 (NPNF, 2nd Series, 1:127).

25. See B. Reicke, ed. and trans., *The Epistles of James, Peter, and Jude,* Anchor Bible (New York: Doubleday, 1964), p. xv, who dates it in the 90s; see also Martin Dibelius, *A Commentary on the Epistle of James:,* Heinrich Greeven, Hermenia Series (Philadelphia: Fortress, 1976), p. 45, who places it somewhere between A.D. 80–130; cf. Sophie Laws, *A Commentary on the Epistle of James* (San Francisco: Harper & Row, 1980), pp. 39–41.

26. See notes 29 and 30 below for proponents of this position.

27. See note 31 below for proponents of this position.

28. We should possibly mention here further reasons why some scholars (see esp. Guthrie, pp. 761–64, and Sidebottom, pp. 13–16, 18) date the epistle early. First, A.D.

70 is a natural *terminus ad quem* because the epistle is silent on the destruction of Jerusalem and it is unlikely that a Christian writer would have ignored such a catastrophe. However, we must contend that this is an argument from silence. Second, there is not a strong rabbinical influence, as for instance in Matthew, and that tradition seems to have reached its final form after the destruction of the city (cf. esp. Sidebottom, p. 15, for this argument); this, therefore, points to an earlier stage in the tradition which James shared with Matthew. Third, there are hardly any allusions to religious persecution, and if those passages which speak of persecution are insisted upon as referring to religious persecution, it would be best understood as the persecution which followed Stephen's death, not that of the turn of the century. Fourth, the epistle infers a primitive church order, as well as a lack of false teachings and heresies in the church, such as a nascent Gnosticism—a phenomenon which characterized the later communities and the later writings. Fifth, Gerald H. Randall points out that the economic conditions mentioned in the document, which portrays "large land-holders preying upon a burdened peasantry, came to an end with the Jewish War" *(The Epistle of St. James and Judaic Christianity* [Cambridge: Cambridge University Press, 1964], p. 32).

29. F. J. A. Hort, *The Epistle of James* (London: MacMillan, 1909), pp. xxiv–xxv; cf. Sidebottom, pp. 16–18. Randall, p. 87, reverses the argument and makes Paul (esp. in Romans) dependent on James, thus dating James between A.D. 49 (A.D. 48 being the earliest date for Galatians, in which no evidence of familiarity with James is found) and A.D. 55 (A.D. 56 being the date of Romans). This, of course, is also as much a misunderstanding as the reverse argument.

30. R. V. G. Tasker, *The General Epistle of James,* vol. 16 of the Tyndale New Testament Commentaries (Grand Rapids: Eerdmans, 1976), p. 31. Of course the argument for lack of doctrine can also be used by those who argue for a much earlier date, the point being that a lack of doctrine implies an immaturity of development.

31. This position is supported by Joseph B. Mayor, *The Epistle of James: The Greek Text with Introduction and Notes and Comments,* 2nd ed. (Grand Rapids: Baker Book House, 1978), pp. cxxi–xliii; R. J. Knowling, *The Epistle of James,* Westminster Commentaries (London: Mathen, 1922), pp. lxviii–lxxii; Gerhard Kittel, "Die Stellung des Jakobus zu Judentum und Heidenchristentum," *Zeitschrift für die Neutestamentliche Wissenschaft (ZNW)* 30 (1931): 145–57; idem, "Der geschichtliche Ort Jakobusbriefes," *ZNW* 41 (1942): 71–105; idem, "Der Jakobusbrief und die Apostolischen Väter," *ZNW* 43 (1950–51): 54–112; Guthrie, p. 764; Robinson, pp. 137–39; cf. also L.E. Elliot-Binns, *Galilean Christianity* (Chicago: Alec R. Allenson, 1956), pp. 46–48; A. Feuillet, 'Le Sens du mot Parouise dans l'Evangile de Matthieu. Comparison entre Matth. XXIV et Jac. V, 1–11," in *The Background of the New Testament and Its Eschatology,* eds. W. D. Davies and D. Daube (Cambridge, Eng.: Cambridge University Press, 1956), pp. 261–80. We can note here that Theodor H. Gaster in the first edition of *The Dead Sea Scriptures* (New York: Doubleday, 1956), p. 15, comes to the conclusion that James is the earliest epistle in the New Testament by comparing it with the Dead Sea Scrolls. He assumes that the scrolls "would have struck a sympathetic chord" in James's community. He claims that it is possible to detect in the epistle "several direct echoes of ideas and expressions prominent in the Qumran texts."

32. Kittel, "Der geschichtliche Ort," p. 82. Robinson, pp. 137–38, also notes that the lack of reference to the controversy over circumcision as well as the terms of the Gentile admission do presuppose a date prior to the council. We could also mention that Feuillet, p. 279, presents an eschatological reason for a very early date. He notes: "We are . . . in the presence of a manner of archaic speaking previous to the period where the Pauline prediction had imposed on the word Parousia the technical

sense which it subsequently preserved"; for example, for James the Parousia has the sense of the historic judgment of the Jewish people.

33. Cf. Malherbe, *Social Aspects,* p. 13.

34. Ibid., pp. 13-14; cf. idem, *The Cynic Epistles: A Study Edition* (Missoula, Mont.: Scholars Press, 1977).

35. See Robinson, p. 122, for an example of one who accepts an early date but argues for a "spiritual Israel" interpretation. We recognize that in later Christian literature the idea of the church as the scattered people of God and sojourners was prominent (see for example, *Epistle to Diognetus* 5 [ANF]; 2 Clem., 5.1, 5, 6 [LCC]; cf. Hermas *Similitude* 9.17 [ANF]; Sidebottom, p. 26). But as is seen below we question whether this is true for the early literature.

36. James B. Adamson, *The Epistle of James,* New International Commentary on the New Testament (Grand Rapids, Mich.: Eerdmans, 1976), pp. 49-50, notes that if James "has a new spiritual meaning for *the twelve tribes* he must not at once add *of the Dispersion,* for this at once anchors it again in the old historical application. The term *of the Dispersion,* here only in the New Testament in the absolute sense [Adamson notes that the force of the article indicates that 'the term is still nontechnical and is used concretely' (p. 49, n.2)], is alive with the ancient, restricted, physical and national privileges of those Jews under the Covenant, and . . . could never have been used by James to symbolize the spiritual catholicity of Christianity."

37. Gerd Theissen, *Sociology,* pp. 35, 42.

38. F. J. Foakes Jackson and Kirsopp Lake, "The Dispersion," in *The Beginning of Christianity, Part I: The Acts of the Apostles,* 5 vols., ed. F. J. Foakes Jackson and Kirsopp Lake (London: MacMillan, 1920), 1:168. However, in the main, Jewish communities were found in Rome, Alexandria, and Antioch; see Josephus *Wars* 8.3.3 (trans. Thackeray, LCL); Leander E. Keck, *The New Testament Experience of Faith* (St. Louis: Bethany, 1976), p. 15; Jackson and Lake, "The Dispersion," pp. 147-48.

39. Feuillet, p. 273. Willibald Beyschlag, *Kritisch-Exegetisches Handbuch über den Brief des Jacobus,* Kritisch Exegetischer Kommentar über das Neue Testament (Göttingen: Vandenhoeck und Ruprecht, 1888), pp. 7-15, argues that the diaspora is outside Palestine, but in James the reference is to a neighboring country of Palestine (probably southern Syria) engaged in much agriculture and commerce.

40. Jackson and Lake, "The Dispersion," p. 147. See also Adamson, p. 50, who also argues that the phrase "the twelve tribes of the dispersion" is not limited to non-Palestinian Jews.

41. Morton Smith, "Palestinian Judaism in the First Century," in *Israel: Its Role in Civilization,* ed. Moshe Davis (New York: Arno, 1977), p. 73.

42. Chapter 1 will propose that Syria and Palestine should probably be viewed as a unit, for this was how it was viewed by the contemporary historians and geographers; cf. Jackson and Lake, "The Dispersion," p. 148.

43. Dikran Y. Hadidian, "Palestinian Pictures in the Epistle of James," *Expository Times* 63 (1951-52): 227-28, presents "a few representative pictures in the Epistle," which he hopes "may serve the reader as pointers toward a Palestinian provenance of the Epistle" (p. 228).

44. "Kräftige persönliche Beteiligung und Leidenschaft," according to Kittel, "Der Geschichtliche Ort," p. 82.

45. Ibid. Cf. Paul H. Furfey, *"Plousios* and Cognates in the New Testament," *The Catholic Biblical Quarterly* 5 (1943): 252; Sidebottom, p. 18. Even Polhill, p. 375, states that a Palestinian origin for the Epistle cannot be ruled out. E. A. Judge, *The Social Pattern of the Christian Groups in the First Century* (London: Tyndale,

1960), p., 53, also notes that James as a Palestinian writing to Israel has received support from the Dead Sea Scrolls. Cf. Gaster, *The Dead Sea Scriptures,* 2nd ed. (1964), p. 17, who argues that it is not unreasonable to conclude that the Dead Sea Scrolls "actually open a window upon the little community of Jewish Christians clustered around James in Jerusalem." For our purposes here it is not necessary to try to discover that exact place in Palestine (or Syro-Palestine) from which the epistle originates. For more on this see Elliott-Binns, pp. 45–46; Hort, pp. xxii–xxiv; and James Hardy Ropes, *A Critical Commentary on The Epistle of St. James,* International Critical Commentary (New York: Charles Scribner's Sons, 1916), p. 49.

46. Schlatter, p. 61.

47. Dibelius, pp. 1–11 and Ropes, pp. 10–16, led the way in contending that the epistle is paraenesis and should be classified with the Greek diatribe, which was an unsystematic form of address with general ethical instructions and exhortations, especially characteristic of Cynics. Harold S. Songer, in "The Literary Character of the Book of James," *Review and Expositor* 66 (1969), has also championed this view. He notes that "paraenetic literature is characterized by a lack of development of thought." James is characterized by "juxtaposing exhortations without concern to develop one theme or one line of thought in the entire epistle." Thus it cannot be made to relate to a specific historical situation. "The book is a collection of ethical maxims and exhortations which cannot be related to a single Christian community or unified Christian situation" (pp. 383, 384); cf. Polhill, p. 372, who though arguing that James has no specific theological teaching or social situation in mind states that it would be erroneous to classify the epistle as Stoic diatribe (or as Jewish Wisdom literature). It is characteristic of paraenesis that it borrowed widely, he contends. Cf. also Sidebottom, pp. 1–3, who holds to the opinion that James shares some of the characteristics of the diatribe style and feels that "the case for comparison with the diatribe has been made out" (p.2). We should note here the caution of Malherbe, who warns against lumping Stoic diatribe and Cynic diatribe together. He notes that "the picture of Cynicism that emerges from [the Cynics'] letters is of rich diversity that compels us to be more circumspect in using the Stoic writers as authorities on Cynicism" *(The Cynic Epistles,* p. 3).

48. See Adamson, p. 11, who claims that one of his chief aims is to combat the error that the epistle lacks cohesion of thought or design. Interestingly, although Bo Reicke does not argue for cohesion in James, he challenges the form-critical understanding of the composition of the document. He writes: "The reason for the apparent lack of system in the Epistle of James is not, as some hold, that the author has collected admonitions and sayings from various sources at random without reworking and classifying them. The order of the material is rather dependent on the the conditions current in the communities which stir and trouble the author" *(Epistles,* p. 7).

49. Ph.D. Dissertation (University of Manchester, 1974), cited in Peter H. Davids, "Theological Perspectives on the Epistle of James," *The Journal of the Evangelical Theological Society* 23 (1980): 97; cf., his *Epistle,* pp. 34ff.

50. See Sidebottom, pp. 21–22, who suggests that the theological message of James is "the overcoming of evil and relief from trouble." Cf. Shepherd, p. 43, who states that "James's stress is not upon afflictions suffered for the sake of Christian discipleship, but upon the ordinary trials and sufferings of life, and in particular the oppression of the poor by the rich"; see also Theodor Zahn, "Die Sociale Frage und die Innere Mission nach dem Brief des Jakobus," *Zeitschrift für Kirchliche Wissenschaft und Kirchlisches Leben* 10 (1889): 298–99; Ralph P. Martin, "The Life-Setting of the Epistle of James in the Light of Jewish History," *Biblical and Near Eastern Studies: Essays in Honor of William Sanford Lasor,* ed. Gary A. Tuttle (Grand

Rapids: Eerdmans, 1978), pp. 97–103; and Sidebottom, p.23. It has been brought to my atention that Francis Xavier Kelley wrote a Ph.D dissertation on the theme of Poor and Rich in James. The information came too late, however, for me to obtain that work and include insights from it in this work.

CHAPTER 1

1. See M. Rostovtzeff, *The Social and Economic History of the Hellenistic World,* 3 vols. (Oxford: Clarendon, 1941), 2:1301, 1308; idem, *The Social and Economic History of the Roman Empire,* rev. P. M. Frazer, 2 vols. (Oxford: Clarendon, 1957), 1:91.

2. See Ramsay MacMullen, *Roman Social Relations: 50 B.C. to A.D. 284* (New Haven: Yale University Press, 1974), p. 89. He, however, claims that statistically there was a middle class. At the top of the social pyramid stood the aristocracy, which included the extremely prominent and rich nobility; at the bottom was a large mass of the totally indigent, both free and slave; in the middle was a heterogeneous variety, which was too dissimilar to be called a middle class. Robin Scroggs in "The Earliest Christian Communities as Sectarian Movement," in *Christianity, Judaism and Other Greco-Roman Cults: Studies for Morton Smith at Sixty,* 4 vols., ed. Jacob Neusener (Leiden: E. J. Brill, 1975), 2:9, also argues that there was scarcely a middle class at all. However, he suggests that "some trading, a small fishing industry, scattered artisans, and a few government officials composed the middle class." Cf. Joachim Jeremias, *Jerusalem in the Time of Jesus: An Investigation into Economic and Social Conditions during the New Testament Period* (Philadelphia: Fortress, 1969), chap. 5, "The Middle Class," where he points to the small industrialist or craftsperson who was independent and did not hire out as a member of the middle class. However, he states that "we rarely come across evidence for the economic situation of this class" (p. 100). Martin Hengel, *Property and Riches in the Early Church: Aspects of a Social History of Early Christianity* (Fortress, 1974), p. 37, also takes the line that "the majority of early Christians will have belonged to the 'middle class' of antiquity." Interestingly, however, on the next page Hengel states that "Paul himself says that the communities were predominantly poor and we have no reason for mistrusting him" (cf. 2 Cor. 8:2). See also Malherbe, *Social Aspects,* p. 86.

3. Rostovtzeff, *The Hellenistic World,* 2:113; cf. pp. 852–53.

4. See Samuel Dickey, "Some Economic and Social Conditions of Asia Minor affecting the Expansion of Christianity," in *Studies in Early Christianity,* ed. Shirley Jackson Case (New York: Century, 1928), p. 395; cf. Rostovtzeff, *The Roman Empire,* 1:3.

5. Rostovtzeff, *The Hellenistic World,* 1:430, 455–64.

6. Ibid., pp. 491–502. Rostovtzeff, however, notes that much of the territory (probably the greater part) remained in the hands of the natives.

7. Martin Hengel, *Judaism and Hellenism: Studies in their Encounter in Palestine during the Early Hellenistic Period* (London: SCM, 1974), 1:56–57; see pp. 32–55 for details of conditions; cf. Frederick C. Grant, *The Economic Background of the Gospels* (New York: Russel & Russel, 1973), p. 69; H. C. Kee, *Community of the New Age* (Philadelphia: Westminster, 1977), p. 79.

8. See Rostovtzeff, *The Roman Empire,* 1:75, 91.

9. William White, Jr., "Finance," in *The Catacombs and the Colosseum: The Roman Empire as the Setting of Primitive Christianity,* ed. Stephen Benko and John H. O'Rourke (Valley Forge, Penn.: Judson, 1971), p. 219.

10. Rostovtzeff, *The Roman Empire,* 1:279; see also pp. 273–75.

11. Victor A. Tcherikover, "Prolegomena," in *Corpus Papyrorum Judaicarum,* ed. Tcherikover, A. Fuks and M. Stern (Cambridge, Mass.: Harvard University Press, 1957), 1:48, translates this "the capitalists lost their deposits."

12. The fact that Philo mentions *geōrgoi* as among the classes in Alexandria makes doubtful the argument of Rostovtzeff that the new Greek settlers were *not* tillers of the soils (*geōrgoi)* but landowners (*geouchoi)* (Rostovtzeff, *The Roman Empire,* 1:282–83). Of course Rostovtzeff clearly states "Greek settlers" while Philo is speaking of Jewish people. Yet it is difficult to make a distinction in terms of economic way of life between these immigrants. The fact remains, however, that they toiled for the king.

13. Philo, *Flaccus* 8 (trans. Colson, LCL).

14. Strabo *Geography* 16. 2.1–2 (trans. Jones, LCL).

15. Mishnah *Shebiith* (6:2).

16. C. F. M. Heichelheim, "Roman Syria," in *An Economic Survey of Ancient Rome,* 6 vols. (Baltimore: Johns Hopkins Press, 1933–40), 4:123; Salo Wittmayer Baron, *A Social and Religious History of the Jews* (New York: Columbia University Press, 1952), 1:258; Jeremias, *Jerusalem,* p. 27.

17. White, p. 230; cf. A. H. M. Jones, "The Urbanization of Palestine," *Journal of Roman Studies* 21 (1938): 78–85. Baron, 1:258, notes that "this southeastern corner of the Mediterranean was economically the most advanced region of the Roman Empire."

18. Gerd Theissen, *Sociology of Early Palestinian Christianity* (Philadelphia: Fortress, 1978), p. 45.

19. White, pp. 229–31; cf. Theissen, *Sociology,* p. 42. Theissen also notes that "the size of the diaspora shows how great emigration must have been. Jews were driven abroad as mercenaries, slaves, fugitives or penniless men in search of a new basis for existence" (p. 35).

20. Mishnah *Nedarim* 9.10. Although statements like these must be read in light of the dramatic changes produced by the catastrophies of A.D. 70 and 135, as well as the famines such as that in A.D. 48, they must also be read in light of the exploitative and oppressive economic situation at that time.

21. John G. Gager, "Religion and Social Class in the Early Roman Empire," in *The Catacombs and the Colosseum: The Roman Empire as the Setting of Primitive Christianity* (Valley Forge, Penn.: Judson, 1971), p. 102.

22. See Louis Finkelstein, *The Pharisees: The Sociological Background of Their Faith,* 2 vols. (Philadelphia: The Jewish Publications Society of America, 1938), for illustrations of the fact that no treatment of the social question in Jewish Palestine is possible apart from the religious setting.

23. See Hugo Mantel, "Sanhedrin," *Encyclopedia Judaica* (1971), 14: 836; cf. David M. Rhoads, *Israel in Revolution: 6–74 C.E.: A Political History Based on The Writings of Josephus* (Philadelphia: Fortress, 1976), pp. 150–53.

24. See Rostovtzeff, *The Roman Empire,* 1:270.

25. See Shirley Jackson Case, *The Social Origins of Christianity* (Chicago: University of Chicago Press, 1923), pp. 87–94.

26. Ernst Troeltsch, *The Social Teaching of the Christian Churches* (New York: Harper & Brothers, 1960), 1:39.

27. Finkelstein, *Pharisees,* 1:36–40.

28. Case, *Social Origins,* pp. 86–87.

29. See Arthur R. Hands, *Charities and Social Aid in Greece and Rome* (New York: Cornell University Press, 1968), p. 117. It must be recognized that the opportunities were greater among the Jews than among the rest of the Roman world because of the Jewish philosophy of education. However, as was mentioned earlier,

the tensions between the scholar and the *'am ha-'aretz* demonstrate that the problem existed to some degree even among the Jews.

30. Cited in MacMullen, *Roman Social Relations,* p.30.

31. See Malherbe, *Social Aspects,* pp. 41-45; cf. John G. Gager, *Kingdom and Community: The Social World of Early Christianity* (Englewood Cliffs, N.J.: Prentice-Hall, 1975) pp. 106-8; and Edwin A. Judge, "The Early Christians as a Scholastic Community," *Journal of Religious History* 1 (1960-61): 4-15, 125-37.

32. Not Christianity in general, as Malherbe suggests, *Social Aspects,* p. 63. He, however, notes that "much remains to be done in working out the points of contact between the church and urban society as reflected in the New Testament." Cf. Ramsay MacMullen, *Enemies of the Roman Order: Treason, Unrest, and Alienation in the Empire* (Cambridge, Mass.: Harvard University Press, 1966), esp. chap. 5; idem, *Roman Social Relations,* chap. 2 and 3; Wayne Meeks, "The Urban Environment of Pauline Christianity," *Society of Biblical Literature 1980 Seminar Papers* (Chico, Calif.: Scholars Press, 1980), pp. 113-22. See Martin Hengel, "Zwischen Jesus und Paulus: Die 'Hellenisten' die 'Sieben' und Stephanus (App. 6, 1-15; 7,54-8,3)," *Zeitschrift für Theologie und Kirche* 72 (1975): 151-206, esp. p. 200, for the role played by the Hellenists in making Christianity a religion of the cities; cf. E. A. Judge, *The Social Patterns of the Christian Groups in the First Century* (London: Tyndale, 1960), pp. 7-17.

33. See Grant, *Economic Background,* p. 7.

34. See Gerd Theissen, 'Soziale Schichtung in der Korinthischen Gemeinde. Ein Beitrag zur Soziologie des hellenistschen Urchristentums," *Zeitschrift für die neutestamentlich Wissenschaft* 65 (1974): 269; idem, *Sociology,* pp. 52, 57; cf. idem, "Legitimation und Lebensunterhalt: Ein Beitrag zür Soziologie urchristlicher Missionare," *New Testament Studies* 21 (1975): 196-97, 200-5.

35. Finkelstein, *Pharisees,* 1:24.

36. See Clarence L. Lee, "Social Unrest and Primitive Christianity," in *The Catacombs and Colosseum: The Roman Empire as the Setting for Primitive Christianity* (Valley Forge, Pa.: Judson, 1971), p. 128; cf. Baron, 1:276; Rostovtzeff, *The Roman Empire,* chap. 9 and passim.

37. Morton Smith, "Zealots and Sicarri, Their Origins and Relation," *Harvard Theological Review* 64 (1971): 17-19; cf. Shimon Applebaum, "Judea as a Roman Province: The Countryside as a Political and Economic Factor," in *Aufgstieg und Niedergang der Römischen Welt: Geschichte und Kultur Roms im Spiegel der Neueren Forschung,* ed. Hildegard Temporini and Wolfgang Haase (Berlin: Walter de Gruyter, 1972-79), 8:372; Rhoads, pp. 150-73.

CHAPTER 2

1. There is not much problem with the term for rich—see Friedrich Hauck and Wilhelm Kasch, *"ploutos"* etc., *Theological Dictionary of the New Testament* (Grand Rapids: Eerdmans, 1964-76), 6:323, where they devote a very brief paragraph to the linguistic data, none of which seem to pose any problem.

2. See Ernst Bammel, *"ptōchos," Theological Dictionary of the New Testament,* 6 :888-89; Thomas Hoyt, Jr., "The Poor in Luke-Acts," Ph.D. Dissertation (Duke University, 1974), pp. 14-15; Francis Brown, S. R. Driver, and Charles Briggs, *A Hebrew and English Lexicon of the Old Testament* (Oxford: Clarendon, 1907).

3. In the LXX, *'ani* is also translated as *penēs,* as well as *tapeinos, praus,* and *asthenēs."* Interestingly, Paul H. Furfey, *"Plouios* and Cognates in the New Testament, " *Catholic Biblical Quarterly* 5 (1943): 245, indicates that in Greek society, by the end of the fourth century, the *penēs* was different from the *ptōchos;* the latter was

the penniless poor person while the former was the working person. Thus when distinguishing the *hoi plousioi* and the *hoi penētes,* Furfey feels the best translation would be "the bourgeoisie" and "the working class," respectively.

4. Robert J. Karris, "The Lukan *Sitz im Leben:* Methodology and Prospects," *Society of Biblical Literature 1976 Seminar Papers* (Missoula, Mont.: Scholars Press, 1976), p. 230n.7.

5. Meinrad Stenzel, "Poverty," in *Baker Encyclopedia of Biblical Theology* (Grand Rapids, Mich.: Baker, 1970), 2:671-72; Bammel, p. 889; cf. Augustin George, "Poverty in the Old Testament," in *Gospel Poverty: Essays in Biblical Theology* (Chicago: Franciscan Herald, 1977), p. 7, who calls the Mosaic time a period of "collective poverty in the economic sense."

6. Roland de Vaux, *Ancient Israel* (New York: McGraw-Hill, 1965), 1:173, suggests that the growth of pauperism in Israel was due to the "alienation of family property and the development of lending at interest." He further states that "this destroyed the social equality which had existed at the time of the tribal federation and which still remained as an ideal." To remedy these evils the institution of the Sabbatical and Jubilee years was legislated.

7. See "The Poor in Luke-Acts," p. 31.

8. Julian Morgenstern, *Amos Studies* (Cincinnati: Hebrew Union College Press, 1941), 1:403, cited in Hoyt "The Poor in Luke-Acts," p. 33.

9. See also Amos 2:6-8; 4:1-3; 5:11-13.

10. Cf. Bammel, p. 893. Stenzel, p. 672, is more blunt in writing that "only in the rational speculation of the proverbial literature do we find instances here and there of a man becoming poor through his own fault"; cf. Hoyt, "The Poor in Luke-Acts," pp. 44-46. Hoyt cites and tends to disagree with Robert Gordis, "The Social Background of Wisdom Literature," *Hebrew Union College Annual* 18 (1943-44): 77-118, who suggests that the reason for the positive view of the wealthy in this literature and the depreciation of the poor is the fact that the sages were products of the upper class.

11. See Prov. 6:6-11, 10:4; 12:11; 13:18; 14:23; 19:15; 20:13; 21:5, 17; 23:20, 21; 24:33, 34; 28:19, 22.

12. Prov. 10:4, 15; 14:20; 18:11; 19:4; 22:7.

13. Cf. Prov. 19:22; 28:6.

14. Prov. 10:2; 11:28; 13:11; 15:6; 21:6; 23:45; 28:8.

15. Prov. 11:24, 25; 19:17; 21:13; 22:9, 16; 28:27; 31:9. N.B., Job points to his attitude of compassion and justice on behalf of the poor as an evidence of his integrity—29:15, 16; 31:16-23; cf. J. W. MacGorman, "Introducing the Book of James, " *Southwestern Journal of Theology* 12 (1969): 20.

16. Pss. 9:12, 18; 10:2, 9, 17; 12:5; 14:66; 34:6; 35:10; 40:17; 68:10; 70:5; 82:1-4; 107:41; 109:31; 113:7-18; 140:12; 145:14-16, etc.

17. Pss. 14:5-6; 34:9, 15-22; 37:14; 132:15, 16; 146:7.

18. Pss. 10:3-11; 31:16; 35:10; 37:14, 16; 94:3-7; 109 and passim.

19. Cf. Hoyt, "The Poor in Luke-Acts," pp. 47-51; Bammel, pp. 891-93; Martin Dibelius, *James: A Commentary on the Epistle of James* (Philadelphia: Fortress, 1976), p. 39.

20. See 1 Enoch 103:105. Interestingly 2 Bar. 70 does not put the "reversal" in the life to come but within this life. Thus it says, "those who were nothing shall rule over the strong, and the poor shall have abundance beyond the rich" (70:4); Martin Hengel, *Property and Riches in the Early Church: Aspects of a Social History of Early Christianity* (Philadelphia: Fortress, 1974), p. 18.

21. See, e.g., Testament of Issachar 3:8; 4:2; 5:2; 7:5; Testament of Zebulum 6:4-7; 8:1-3; Testament of Joseph 3:5; Testament of Benjamin 4:1.

22. See, e.g., Sir. 13:24; 18:32-19:3; 31:8; 40:18.

23. See, e.g., Sir. 8:2; 10:31; 11:19; 13:3–7, 19–23; 26:29; 27:11; 34: 20–22.

24. See Louis Finkelstein, *The Pharisees: The Sociological Background of Their Faith,* 2 vols. (Philadelphia: The Jewish Publications Society of America, 1938), 1:4–5, for a suggestive sociological depiction of the strata of Jewish Palestine during this period.

25. See Hoyt, "The Poor in Luke-Acts," p. 81; note also Josephus *Antiquities* 13.5.9; 18.1.4, and *Wars* 2.8.14, for their theology; cf. Hauck and Kasch, "ploutos," p. 325; J. Jeremias, *Jerusalem in the Time of Jesus* (Philadelphia: Fortress, 1969), pp. 95–99, 228–32.

26. See, e.g., B. Talmud *Pesahim* 496; cf. Mishnah *Aboth* 2:6.

27. Seneca *Epistle* 90.37; cf. W. E. Heitland, *Agricola: A Study of Agriculture and Rustic Life in the Graeco-Roman World from the Point of View of Labor* (Cambridge, Eng.: Cambridge University Press, 1921), p. 248.

28. Salo Wittmayer Baron, *A Social and Religious History of the Jews* (New York: Columbia University Press, 1952), 1:259.

29. Ibid.

30. Josephus *Wars* 2.8.3; cf. *Antiquities* 18.1.5; Philo *Every Good Man Is Free* 12.

31. See 1Qs. 6:13–7:8; CD 6:11–7:6a (trans. Gaster, *Dead Sea Scriptures,* 2nd ed.); cf. William R. Farmer, "The Economic Basis of the Qumran Community," *Theologische Zeitschrift (TZ)* 11 (1955): 295–308; and the follow-up article, "A Postscript to the Economic Basis of the Qumran Community," *TZ* 12 (1956): 56–58.

32. Cf. Leander E. Keck, "The Poor among the Saints in Jewish Christianity and Qumran," *Zeitschrift für die neutestamentliche Wissenschaft* 57 (1966): 54–78.

33. Mark can hardly be said to have a systematic teaching on the subject. Peter Davids, however, has shown that the Gospel does present the poor favorably, as in the pericopes regarding the widow's mite (12:41–44), the anointing at Bethany (14:3–9), and the call of the first disciples (1:16–20). But Davids notes that "these form no developed theology about wealth" ("The Poor Man's Gospel," *Themelios* 1 [1976]: 37n. 1); cf. pp. 37–38.

34. Robert J. Karris, "Missionary Communities: A New Paradigm for the Study of Luke-Acts," *Catholic Biblical Quarterly* 41 (1979): 89; he admits, however, that "the scholarly dust has not yet settled on the highly important question of the extent to which Luke devotes time and energy to real problems caused by rich folks in his communities" (ibid.).

35. See Larimore Clyde Crockett, "The Old Testament in the Gospel of Luke: With Emphasis on the Interpretation of Isaiah 61:1–2," 2 vols., Ph.D. Dissertation (Brown University, 1966), pp. 351–55; Luke T. Johnson, *The Literary Function of Possessions in Luke-Acts* (Missoula, Mont.: Scholars Press, 1977), pp. 130–141; Karl Holl, *Gesammelte Aufsätze zur Kirchengeschichte,* 3 vols. (Tübingen: J.C.B. Mohr, 1928).

36. See Hoyt, "The Poor in Luke-Acts," pp. v, 246; Leander E. Keck, "The Poor among the Saints in the New Testament," *Zeitschrift für die neutestamentlic Wissenschaft* 56 (1965): 109–10; Joachim Jeremias, *The Parables of Jesus,* rev. ed. (New York: Charles Scribner's Sons, 1963), pp. 65–96; Jacques Duponto, "The Poor and Poverty in the Gospels and Acts," in *Gospel Poverty: Essays in Biblical Theology* (Chicago: Franciscan Herald Press, 1977), p. 27; David Bosch, *Witness to the World: The Christian Mission Perspective* (Atlanta: John Knox, 1980), p. 217, notes that the interpretation "by evangelicals" of "poor" in the Gospels as indicating "spiritual poor" is "a convenient heresy, the fruit of centuries-old docetism and Monophysitism, and mutiliation of the gospel. It is a message of cheap grace, where the materially rich join the ranks of the spiritually poor with the greatest of ease, thus

eluding the summons to conversion in respect of possessions and life-style."

37. We, like Karris, "The Lukan *Sitz im Leben,*" p. 229, disassociate our definition of the poor from Joachim Jeremias, *New Testament Theology: The Proclamation of Jesus* (New York: Charles Scribner's Sons, 1971) p. 113, who sees them as 'the hungry, those who weep, the sick, those who labor, . . . the last, the lost, the sinners." This definition is too broad and is not contextually supported.

38. See Jeremias, *New Testament Theology,* p. 112; W. D. Davies, *The Setting of the Sermon on the Mount* (Cambridge, Eng.: Cambridge University Press, 1964), p. 251; Duponto, pp. 37–38; cf. D. Flusser, "Blessed are the Poor in Spirit . . . ," *Israel Exploration Journal* 10 (1960): 11.

39. 1QH 18:14–15 (trans. Dupont-Sommer); cf. 1Qm 14:7.

40. Flusser, pp. 1–13, esp. p. 9; Davies, p. 251, disagrees and states that to pin down the phrase to the sectarians is unwarranted. He argues that the fact that its Hebrew equivalent appears in the scroll only proves its Palestinian origin and writes: "The term 'poor,' rightly understood in v.3 as 'poor in spirit,' has a religious even more than a social and economic connotation in Judaism which need not be confined to the Essenes." Cf. Neil J. McEleny, "The Beatitudes of the Sermon on the Mount/Plain," *Catholic Biblical Quarterly* 43 (1981): 5–6.

41. See citation from Davies in preceding note.

42. Flusser, p. 6.

43. Ibid. Keck, "The Poor among the Saints in Jewish Christianity," pp. 71–72, disagrees with this interpretation by Flusser.

44. Keck, "The Poor among the Saints in the New Testament," p. 116.

45. Nils Abstrup Dahl, *Jesus in the Memory of the Early Church* (Minneapolis: Augsburg, 1976), p. 91. See Richard Cassidy, "The Social and Political Stance of Jesus in Luke's Gospel," Ph.D. Dissertation (Graduate Theological Union, 1976); and his book *Jesus, Politics, and Society: A Study of Luke's Gospel* (Maryknoll, N.Y.: Orbis, 1978), pp. 20–49, for a good overview of the social stance of Jesus in Luke. Much of our summary is based on Cassidy's outline.

46. Note also again the blessing to the poor and the woe to the rich in the Great Sermon of chap. 6.

47. Robert M. Grant, *Early Christianity and Society* (San Francisco: Harper & Row, 1977), p. 97.

48. Karris, "The Lukan *Sitz im Leben,*" p. 222, presupposes that Acts 2:41–47 and 4:31–35 "opens the window onto the Sitz im Leben behind the Lukan theme of poor and rich." See Peter Davids, "The Poor Man's Gospel," *Themelios* 1 (1976): 40, who notes that Acts is Luke's answer to the question, How should the teachings of Jesus as presented in the Gospel work in practice?

49. See John G. Gager, *Kingdom and Community: The Social World of Early Christianity* (Englewood Cliffs, N.J.: Prentice-Hall, 1975), p. 25.

50. Hengel, *Property and Riches,* p. 35, suggests two reasons why we do not come across this sharing of goods in the Pauline mission communities: firstly, "the tension of the expectation of an imminent end was relaxed in favor of the task of worldwide mission, and secondly, that in the long run the form of 'love communism' practiced in Jerusalem was not possible. It was impossible to maintain a sharing of goods in a free form without the kind of fixed organization and common production which we find, say, at Qumran. . . . Free, charismatic community rather than a legalistic idea of order is typical of primitive Christianity."

51. Cf. Gal. 2:10 (a request by the Jerusalem church to remember the poor) and Rom. 15:26 (a reference to the poor at Jerusalem). Philip Seidensticker, "St. Paul and Poverty," in *Gospel Poverty: Essays in Biblical Theology* (Chicago: Franciscan Herald Press, 1977), argues that the idea of *ptōchos* in these passages does not

"primarily include the element of economic and social necessity" (p. 92); rather, it is close to the biblical spirituality of the Palestinian Jews' "idea of the poor" (p. 84). Leander Keck, throughout his entire article "The Poor Among the Saints in the New Testament,' but especially in pp. 117-29, demonstrates that the Pauline material does not provide the needed data for the argument that *hoi ptōchos* is a technical designation of the church which felt itself especially close to God.

52. Gerd Theissen, *The Social Setting of Pauline Christianity* (Philadelphia: Fortress, 1982), passim; and various articles collected in *Studien zür Soziologie des Urchristentums* (Tübingen: J. C. B. Mohr, 1979).

53. E. A. Judge, *The Social Pattern of the Christian Groups in the First Century* (London: Tyndale, 1960), p. 60, says that the Corinthian Christian community was "dominated by a socially pretentious section of the population of the big cities"; cf. Karris, "Missionary Communities," pp. 87-88.

54. See Robin Scroggs, "Paul and the Eschatological Woman," *Journal of the American Academy of Religion* 40 (1972): 283-303, where he shows how the relation between men and women demonstrates a basic egalitarianism existing within the early Christian communites; cf. Wayne A. Meeks, "The Image of the Androgyne: Some Uses of a Symbol in Earliest Christianity," *History of Religions* 13 (1973-74): 165-208; Elizabeth Schüssler Fiorenza, " 'You Are Not to Be Called Father': Early Christian History in a Feminist Perspective," *Cross Currents* 29 (1980): 301-3.

55. The data in 1 Cor. proves Ernst Troeltsch, *The Social Teaching of the Christian Churches* (New York: Harper & Brothers, 1960), 1:39, and Gustavo Gutiérrez and Richard Shaull, *Liberation and Change* (Atlanta: John Knox, 1977), pp. 5-6, wrong when they argue that it was only in the second century that the well-to-do, educated, upper social strata began entering the church. It is, however, correct that for the first two centuries of Christianity the Christian community was essentially composed of the lower class of the empire. Yet when persons of wealth began to enter the church, the church adapted its ideology to meet the new situation. John G. Gager, "Religion and Social Class in Early Roman Empire," in *The Catacombs and the Colosseum* (Valley Forge, Pa.: Judson, 1971), p. 113, illustrates this by showing that God had provided wealth solely for the performance of his ministries, while Clement of Alexandria . . . sought to modify the tradition by showing that only the misuse of money, not money itself, constituted a barrier to salvation"; cf. Carolyn Ann Osiek, "Rich and Poor in the Shepherd of Hermas," (Ph.D. Dissertation (Harvard University, 1978); Shirley Jackson Case, *The Social Triumph of the Ancient Church* (London: George Allen Unwin, 1934), p. 45; L. W. Country-man, *The Rich Christian in the Church of the Early Empire* (New York: Edwin Mellen, 1980), passim. Gager further suggests that one way in which the church dealt with the ideology of poverty "was to institutionalize the ideology in the form of the priesthood and the monastry" *(Kingdom,* p. 112n. 70; cf. p. 106). Quite interesting is the speculation noted by Jean-Luc Blondel that "the difficulty the Letter of James had in gaining canonical recognition may have been because he took the wealthy to task at a time when conciliation with the wealthy was being sought" ("Theology and Paraenesis in James," *Theology Digest* 28 [1980]: 256).

56. Grant, *Early Christianity,* pp. 112-23.

CHAPTER 3

1. Martin Dibelius, *James: A Commentary on the Epistle of James* (Philadelphia: Fortress, 1976), pp. 83-84; cf. W. Robertson Nicoll, *The Expositor's Greek Testament* (Grand Rapids: Eerdmans, 1956), 4:424, who contends that only by

supplying mental, artificial links can a connection be made. He, however, fails to deal with the connective *de.*

2. Dibelius, p. 70.

3. James Hardy Ropes, *A Critical Commentary on the Epistle of St. James* (New York: Charles Scribner's Sons, 1916), p. 144; cf. Burton Scott Easton, "The Epistle of James: Introduction and Exegesis," in the *Interpreter's Bible* (New York: Abingdon, 1957), 12:24; Archibald Thomas Robertson, *Word Pictures in the New Testament* (Nashville: Broadman, 1930–33), 6:15.

4. F. J. A. Hort, *The Epistle of James* (London: MacMillan, 1909), p. 14.

5. Ibid. Hort further states that "poverty, riches, and the change from one to the other may be among the 'ways' in all of which the waverer is found unstable." Cf. E. H. Plumptre, ed., *The General Epistle of St. James, The Cambridge Bible for School and Colleges Series* (Cambridge, Eng.: Cambridge University Press, 1915), p. 51 who suggests that the sequence of ideas between the two verses lies in the fact that the "love of mammon is the most common source of the 'double-mindedness.' " See also A.E. Barnett, "Letter of James," *Interpreter's Dictionary of the Bible* (1962), 2:795, who approaches it from a different angle, viz., making the connection with the concept of wisdom in v. 5: "Joy in the midst of adversity discloses the wisdom God gives. The emphemeral character of riches, discerned by wisdom, is illustrated by flowers that 'fade and die'."

6. Walter Grundmann, *"Tapeinos,* etc." *Theological Dictionary of the New Testament* (Grand Rapids: Eerdmans, 1964–76), 8:1.

7. Ibid., pp. 6–12; cf. Nicoll, 4:425.

8. Cf. Nicoll, 4:425; James B. Adamson, *The Epistle of James* (Grand Rapids: Eerdmans, 1976), p. 62.

9. Cf. David Bartlett, "The Epistle of James as a Jewish-Christian Document," *Society of Biblical Literature 1979 Seminar Papers* (Missoula, Mont.: Scholars Press, 1979), 2:184. Keck, "The Poor among the Saints in the New Testament," *Zeitschrift für die neutestamentliche Wissenschaft* 56 (1965): 117, agrees that the document "presupposes a piety of poor folk," but he is adamant that "this does not mean that the Christians [James] knows called themselves 'The Poor'."

10. Harold S. Songer, "James," *The Broadman Bible Commentary*, 12 vols. (Nashville: Broadman, 1972), 12:109, says "not *primarily* economic." Emphasis added.

11. Cf. Dibelius, pp. 39–45; Carolyn Ann Osiek, "Rich and Poor in the Shepherd of Hermas," Th.D dissertation (Harvard University, 1978), agrees with Dibelius; James Moffatt, *The General Epistles: James, Peter, Judas* (New York: Harper and Row, n.d.), p. 33. Bartlett, "The Epistle of James," p. 184. Although the latter author finds it difficult to judge how the term is used in James, he states that in 1:9–11 the "lowly brother" sounds like the "poor" of the Ps. of Solomon 10:6. Franz Mussner, *Der Jakobusbrief,* Herders Theologischer Kommentar zum Neuen Testament (Freiberg: Herder, 1967), pp. 80–83, argues for a thoroughly religious connotation, "no matter how much the social element concurs also, insofar as the poor from a distance . . . in the epistle are understood as really poor in an economic view" (p. 80); cf. Songer, "James," p. 109.

12. Alfred Plummer, *The General Epistles of St. James and St. Jude,* vol. 29 of *The Expositor's Bible,* 33 vols. (New York: A. C. Amstrong and Son, 1908), p. 81, and Robertson, *Word Pictures,* 6:15, contrast *tapeinos* as used here in the social sense with the same word in Matt. 11:29 which refers to the spiritually humble. Ropes, p. 145, also makes the contrast, but for him it is James 4:6 which deals with the inner spirit; cf. Jean Cantinat, *Les Épîtres de Saint Jacques et de Saint Jude* (Paris: Libraire Lecoffre, 1973), p. 77. Of course the question can be raised whether the term in both those passages has only a spiritual inner significance without any

social element. Cf. also Sophie Laws, *A Commentary on the Epistle of James* (San Francisco: Harper and Row, 1980), p. 62, who shows that the antithetical structure of James 1: 9–11 makes it evident that the *tapeinos* should not be understood spiritually or morally, but socially and materially.

13. Meinrad Stenzel, "Poverty," *Baker Encyclopedia of Biblical Theology* (Grand Rapids, Mich.: Baker, 1970), 2:673, cf. Joseph Chaine, *L'Épîtres de Saint Jacques,* (Paris: Librairie Lecoffre, 1927), p. 14, who states that "James does not represent here a theme of 'the literature of the poor' which rough-handles *[Malmème]* the rich (contra Dibelius), but he expresses a very beautiful thought of spirituality."

14. Cf. Adamson, p. 62.

15. It could be argued that *ho tapeinos* parallels *tēi tapeinosei,* but the antithesis does not seem to allow it.

16. Dibelius, p. 87.

17. Ropes, pp. 145–46; cf. Adamson, p. 30, who claims that in v. 10 the rich person is a Christian, but in v. 11 "the rich" is a generic term; see also Joseph B. Mayor, *The Epistle of James: The Greek Text with Introduction and Notes and Comments,* 2nd ed. (Grand Rapids, Mich.: Baker, 1978), pp. 43–44, who argues for the heroic viewpoint and asks, "How could one who had known Nicodemus and Mary of Bethany, Joseph of Arimathaea and Barnabas, have thus denied to the rich the privilege of Christian membership?" But Mayor and many expositors from the second century until now have failed to take note of the fact that these rich persons, when they became part of the Jesus movement, shared their wealth and had "all things in common" (Acts 2:44; 4:32) with the other Christians. Thus they no longer belonged to the category called "the rich." For a point of view similar to Mayor's, see C. Leslie Milton, *The Epistle of James* (Grand Rapids: Eerdmans, 1966), pp. 36–37; Thomas W. Leahy, "The Epistle of James," *The Jerome Biblical Commentary* (Englewood Cliifs, N.J.: Prentice-Hall, 1968), p. 371; R.C.H. Lenski, *The Interpretations of the Epistle to the Hebrews and the Epistle of James* (Columbus, Ohio: Wartburg, 1946), pp. 534–35; Theodor Zahn, "Die Sociale Frage und die Innere Mission nach dem Brief des Jakobus," *Zeitschrift für Kirchliche Wissenschaft und Kirchliches Leben* 10 (1889): 298–99.

18. Ropes, p. 146.

19. Easton, p.25.

20. Nicoll, 4:424–25.

21. Ropes, p. 146.

22. Nicoll, 4:424.

23. Dibelius, p. 85; cf. Songer, "James," p. 109; Walter Bauer, *A Greek-English Lexicon of the New Testament and Other Early Christian Literature,* 2nd ed., rev. F. Wilbur Gingrich and Frederick W. Danker (Chicago: University of Chicago Press, 1979), p. 805. See also Plummer, *The General Epistles,* p. 82, who states that "it is a baseless assumption to suppose that the rich man here spoken of is a Christian at all." He is a wealthy Jew who rejects Christ. Cf. Laws, pp. 63–64.

24. Ropes, p. 146.

25. Ibid.

26. Dibelius, p. 85; cf. E. C. Blackman, *The Epistle of James* (London: SCM, 1957), p. 51.

27. Dibelius, pp. 87–88.

28. R. A. Martin has joined the chorus of those attempting to placate the contemporary wealthy. In his *James* (Minneapolis: Augsburg, 1982) he argues that in this passage the rich who are condemned are "those who draw a sense of security from their wealth and who use their position and power for selfish ends" (p. 22). He

goes on to state categorically that although a "vast majority" of the rich fit that description, not all do. Martin is obviously engaging in eisegesis; he is reading into the passage an interpretation that is clearly not intended by the author. For James, it is not the "vast majority" of the rich of his day who are condemned—it is all of them. See my comments in n. 17 of the present chapter.

29. Cf. Peter Davids, *The Epistle of James: A Commentary on the Greek Text* (Grand Rapids, Mich.: Eerdmans, 1982), p. 77.

30. Cf. Mayor, pp. 43–45; Ropes, p. 145; and Adamson, p. 30, who claim that the rich person in vv. 9–10 is a Christian while "the rich" in v. 11 is a generic term *(qua rich,* according to Mayor) and is not necessarily referring to a Christian, but rather represents the typical rich person. It is difficult to comprehend on what basis such a distinction can be made. Ronald A. Ward, "James," *The New Bible Commentary Revised* (London: Inter-Varsity, 1970), p. 1224, does not make the distinction but claims that both "the lowly one" and "the rich" are generic, referring in each case to a class and not to an individual.

31. Ropes, p. 145, notes that *Kauchaomai* indicates boasting over a privilege or possession: "The word is used in the OT of 'any proud and exulting joy,' and so here."

32. Ropes, pp. 146–47, suggests that this bringing low is through loss of possessions. This he says "might be by reason of his profession, for the rich man was peculiarly exposed to loss in time of persecution."

33. Mussner, p. 76.

34. Cf. Dibelius, p. 84; Blackman, p. 51; Leahy, p. 371; Songer, "James," p.109; Adamson, p. 29; Mussner, p. 76, who all understand it eschatologically.

35. Ropes, p. 145, notes that some make *hupsos* refer to the heavenly reward of the pious. This is included in the meaning of the term, says Ropes, but he goes on to state that the text fails to say that the elevation is to occur solely in the future. He points out that "the exaltation of the humble was the promise of the prophets (e.g. Isa. 54:11ff) and the hope of Israel, Prov. 3:34, Psa. 18:27, 138:6. . . . These are not realized. But note the moralistic turn given to apocalyptic ideas; in 1 Pet. 1:3 the eschatological framework of Jewish and Christian thought is far nearer the surface of the writer's consciousness." Further on Ropes states that the term *maranthēsetai* as used here has reference to the "loss of riches and earthly prosperity, not to eternal destiny" (p. 149). But again we must emphasize that this passage says nothing regarding the possessions of the rich. Cf. Bo Reicke, *The Epistles of James, Peter, and Jude,* The Anchor Bible (New York: Doubleday, 1964), p. 15, who suggests that the concern of the author is over "the readers' preoccupation with the question of wealth"; and Frank Stagg, "Exegetical Themes in James 1 and 2," *Review and Expositor* 66 (1969): 394, who states that the concern of the pericope is to warn "against the uncertainty or transitory character of wealth."

36. Job 14:2; Pss. 37:2; 90:5–6; 103:15; Isa. 40:6–8; 51:12; cf. Dibelius, p. 85. We should note that *anthos chortou* is the LXX rendering of the Hebrew *tists hasadeh* = "flower of the field." Therefore, *chortos* is probably used here of any green herbage, not just grass; see Ropes, pp. 147–48. Cf. Easton, p. 25, who states that the OT imagery of these verses is no evidence that the original author, the editor, or readers of this section were Palestinians.

37. Henry B. Tristram, *The Natural History of the Bible: Being a Review of the Physical Geography, Geology, and Meteorology of the Holy Land; with a Description of Every Animal and Plant Mentioned in Holy Scripture* (London: S.P.C.K., 1880), p. 455; cf. Adamson, p. 63.

38. Bauer, p. 782.

39. Savas C. Agourides, "The Origin of the Epistle of St. James: Suggestions for

a Fresh Approach," *The Greek Orthodox Theological Review* 9 (1963–64): 73; Adamson, p. 63; Ropes, p. 148; Plummer, p. 86; Dikran Y. Hadidian, "Palestinian Pictures in the Epistle of James," *Expository Times* 63 (1951–52): 228. Cf. Bauer, p. 425, who, although recognizing the other usage of *sun,* disagrees that a distinction is made in the verse; in the lexicon Bauer notes that "since the sun brings with it burning heat, but not the scorching east wind, which is usually meant by *kausōn* in the LXX, it is not likely that a hot wind is meant in James' passage" (abbreviated words in the original are spelled out here).

40. Ropes, p. 149.

41. See Adamson, pp. 62–63; cf. Ropes, p. 148; Mayor, p. 44.

42. C. D. F. Moule, *An Idiom Book of New Testament Greek* (Cambridge, Eng.: Cambridge University Press, 1971), p. 12.

43. Robertson, *Word Pictures,* 6:16.

44. Dibelius, pp. 86–87.

45. Ropes, p. 149; cf. Lenski, p. 536. Moule, *An Idiom Book,* p. 209, notes that it is possible that here *"en tais poreiais autou maranthēsetai* might have arisen from a misunderstanding of a Semetic saying in the form of *poreuomenos maranthēsetai."*

46. Cf. Mussner, p. 75; Chaine, p. 16.

47. James Hope Moulton and George Milligan, *The Vocabulary of the Greek Testament* (Grand Rapids: Eerdmans, 1959), p. 528.

48. See Mussner, p. 75. Bauer's lexicon, although agreeing that the plural is a strong indication that the sense of "business journeys" is correct, yet notes that "the pl. may be thought of as parallel to v. 8 *en tais hodois autou"*; thus, that sense cannot be finally excluded (p. 692); cf. Laws, p. 65.

49. See Chaine, p. 16; Hort, p. 18; Moffat, p. 15; Mayor, p. 45; R. V. G. Tasker, *The General Epistle of James* (Grand Rapids, Mich.: Eerdmans, 1976), p. 44.

CHAPTER 4

1. As to the term "affliction"in 1:27, Thomas Hanks, *God So Loved The Third World* (Maryknoll, N.Y.: Orbis, 1983) pp. 46, 47, notes that *thlīpsis* (usually translated "affliction") should be given its primary meaning, "oppression." The softer and more ambiguous terms such as "affliction" and "suffering" lessen the impact of James's alignment with the oppressed. As to the links between 2:17 and earlier passages, see James Hardy Ropes, *A Critical and Exegetical Commentary on the Epistle of St. James* (New York: Charles Scribner's Sons, 1916), p. 185, who states that "in 2:1–7 the thought of the supreme importance of conduct, stated in 1:26–27, is further illustrated by an instance from a situation of common occurrence. With this instance the writer connects his reply to two excuses or pretexts (vv.8–13, 14–26), which are perversions of true religion." See E. Malcolm Sidebottom, *James, Jude, and 2 Peter* (Greenwood, S.C.: Attic, 1967), p. 37, who also connects 2:1–7 with the passage that precedes it by stating that chap. 2 "continues the emphasis upon deeds as against formal religious observance"; cf. Alfred Plummer, *The General Epistles of St. James and St. Jude* (New York: A. C. Armstrong and Son, 1908), p. 117. James B. Adamson, *The Epistle of James* (Grand Rapids, Mich.: Eerdmans, 1976), carries the connection back to 1:9 and sees 2:1–13 as an expansion of the theme in the earlier passage, i.e., the motif of "respect of persons" and the correct relationships between poor and rich in a Christian community: "Respect of persons (2:1) and despising the poor (2:6)," he says, " constitute a denial of Christian brotherhood." This to him is the essential theme of 1:9–10 (p. 102). See also Peter H. Davids, *The Epistle of James: A Commentary on the Greek Text* (Grand Rapids, Mich.: Eerdsmans, 1982), p. 105, who notes that 2:1–13 not only expands 1:9–11 and 1:22–27, but

"forms the basis for the strong denunciation of chaps. 4 and 5."

2. Harold S. Songer, "James," in *The Broadman Bible Commentary,* 12 vols. (Nashville: Broadman, 1972), 12:113-14; Richard L. Scheef, Jr., "The Letter of James," *The Interpreter's One-Volume Commentary on the Bible* (Nashville: Abingdon, 1971), p. 919; cf. Adamson, p. 102.

3. See Roy Bowen Ward, "The Communal Concern of the Epistle of James," Ph.D. Dissertation (Harvard University, 1966), pp. 33-40; cf. Albert Wifstrand, "Stylistic Problems in the Epistles of James and Peter," *Studia Theologica* 1 (1948): 170-82. It may be apropos to note here that the salutation "my brethren" at the beginning of the passage does not necessarily give support to the argument that the audience of the document was a Christian community. The device was rather a common homiletical introduction used both in Judaism and the early Christian church in general (see Davids, *Epistle,* p. 105).

4. Songer, "James," p. 114; cf. Scheef, p. 919. Interestingly, however, we should note that even if this verse should bé taken as a question, it would still not prove that James is utilizing the Greek diatribe style, for as Wifstrand points out, "There are many questions in the book of Job that could be labelled rhetorical" (p. 177).

5. Ropes, p. 186; W. Robertson Nicoll, *The Expositor's Greek New Testament,* 5 vols. (Grand Rapids, Mich.: Eerdmans, 1956), 4:435; Burton Easton, "The Epistle of James," in *The Interpreter's Bible,* 12 vols. (New York: Abingdon, 1957), 12:3.

6. Here *echō* is used with the sense of one's "emotions," "inner possession or quality," etc; cf. James 3:14: "to have jealously" (Henry George Liddel and Robert Scott, *A Greek-English Lexicon,* rev. Henry Stuart Jones [Oxford: Clarendon, 1968], p. 749); Walter Bauer, *A Greek-English Lexicon of the New Testament and Other Early Christian Literature,* 2nd ed., rev. (Chicago: University of Chicago Press, 1979), p. 332. Note *echete* goes both with *pistis* ("faith") as well as *prosōpolēmpsiais.*

7. Cf. Archibald Robertson, *Word Pictures in the New Testament,* 6 vols. (Nashville: Broadman, 1930-33) 6:27, who states it is an exhortation to stop holding *or* not to have the habit of holding in the fashion condemned. See also Sidebottom, p. 37. Adamson feels that it is necessary to add the word "try" to the phrase: "Do not *try* to combine faith in Christ with (let us here say) worship of wealth." To translate the phrase as "Do not combine," he suggests, "would leave men to imagine it would be possible" (p. 102). It seems, however, that such an addition and interpretation is not consonant with the Greek grammar.

8. See also Pss. 82:2, Prov. 6:35; 18:5; Rom. 2:11; Eph. 6:9.

9. Ropes, p. 186, notes that *"en* denotes the state, or condition, in which the act is done; here the acts with which the action of the main verb is accompanied."

10. Cf. Bauer, p. 720; Ropes, p. 185-86.

11. Cf. E. H. Plumptre, ed., *The General Epistle of St. James* (Cambridge, Eng.: The University Press, 1915), p. 63; Ropes, p. 186.

12. *Pistis* ("faith") here is obviously "subjective" faith, not the later concept of a body of doctrine; see Ropes, p. 187.

13. See Davids, *Epistle,* p. 106, for examples.

14. F. J. A. Hort, *The Epistle of St. James* (London: MacMillan, 1909), p. 46.

15. Cf. Ropes, p. 187; Sidebottom, p. 38; Robertson, *Word Pictures,* 6:27, etc.; and the majority of commentators on Romans and Galatians.

16. See Markus Barth, "The Faith of the Messiah, " *Heythrop Journal* 10 (1969): 363-700; George Howard, "Faith of Christ," *Harvard Theological Review* 60 (1967): 459-65; Gabriel Herbert, " 'Faithfulness' and 'Faith'," *Theology* 58 (1955): 373-79; Thomas F. Torrance, "One Aspect of the Biblical Conception of Faith," *Expository Times* 68 (1956): 111-14, with a reply by C. D. F. Moule, "The Biblical

Conception of 'Faith'," *Expository Times* 68 (1956): 157 and Torrance's reply to Moule on pp. 221–22 of the same volume. The RSV translates the phrase as referring to subjective faith. An interesting attempt at interpreting the phrase has been made by Greer M. Taylor, "The Function of *pistis Christou* in Galatians," *Journal of Biblical Literature* 85 (1966): 58–76; Taylor argues that in Galatians Christ's faith is understood in terms of Roman law regarding a *fidei commissum,* and Paul uses the concept, he says, "to explain, in juristic terms, how the inheritance of Abraham is transmitted, through Jesus Christ, both to Jews and gentiles and upon precisely the same terms" (p. 58).

17. Arguing from Galatians, Barth, "Faith of the Messiah," has summarized in 7 points the arguments for this position. The first four are built on "Paul's OT rootage, quotations, allusions and expositions" (p. 367), while the last three are stylistic observations: (1) When Paul illustrates what he means by faith he refers to the OT passages treating of *'emunah* ("faithfulness") and *he'emin* ("to be firm"). Therefore the Pauline word *pistis* has the sense of faithful obedience. (2) In the OT a faithful servant of God is the "instrument by which God carries out the salvation and restoration of his people to obedience and faith" (p. 365). It is thus that, for example, a bad king brought misery over his people, while "a righteous king's obedience means life, salvation, righteousness of a whole people" (p. 366). (3) In contrast to Adam's disobedience stands Christ's obedience, according to Phil. 2:6–8 and Rom. 5:18–19. These references to Christ's obedience are equivalent to references to his faith. (4) The faith of Abraham was instrumental in the blessing God conferred upon Abraham's descendants; the faith of Christ will thus confer much greater blessings upon his followers. (5) Several times Paul places justification by (works of) law in contrast to justification by or in Christ. Thus not only faith in Christ but Christ himself is the alternative to justification by law (cf. Gal. 2:16, 21; 5:4). (6) In Rom. 3:22; Phil. 3:9; Gal. 2:16; 3:22, if *pistis Christou* means faith *in* Christ, the accompanying reference to those who "believe in Christ" would be a "superfluous repetition" (p. 368). (7) Rom. 2:17 and 2 Cor. 5:10 show that Christ is appointed to pass sentence in the final judgment; it follows that justification is no less in Christ's hands than the final judgment. Therefore, while one might have doubts about the certainty of his or her own faith, there is no doubt about the perfect faith of Christ. We should note further two observations made by George Howard, "Faith of Christ," pp. 459–60: (1) In the Pauline corpus the construction of *pistis* followed by the genitive of a person or personal pronouns occurs twenty-four times (not counting *pistis Christou)* and in all cases refers to the faith of the individual, never faith *in* the individual. (2) A peculiar change of idiom in Gal. 2:16 suggests the subjective use of the genitive: "The passage makes a distinction in construction by alternately using the preposition *dia/ek* with the genitive man believing *in* Christ." Thus, for Howard a clear distinction is made here between a person's faith and Christ's faith.

18. Hort, p. 46; cf. p. 47, where he states that "the force . . . of the title here would probably be that the faith of Christ as the glory was peculiarly at variance with favoritism shown to the rich."

19. Cf. Martin Dibelius, *James: A Commentary on the Epistle of James* (Philadelphia: Fortress, 1976), pp. 174–80, as an example of scholars with whom we differ on this point.

20. L. E. Elliot-Binns, "James," in *Peake's Commentary on the Bible* (Hong Kong: Thomas Nelson and Sons, 1962), p. 1023.

21. Ropes, pp. 187–88, gives a total of seven; Dibelius, pp. 127-28, gives three; Adamson, pp. 103–4, presents five different lines of interpretation.

22. Adamson, p. 103.

23. Ibid., p. 104.

24. Davids, *Epistle*, p. 107, points out that Adamson's emendation "appears without basis either in the manuscript evidence or in the given word order. It simply conveniently rearranges the text." Adamson states that he got the idea from P. B. R. Forbes and that it is viewed favorably by F. F. Bruce. The latter wrote in a letter to Forbes: "In support of the transference of 'our' to the end of the sentence—an attractive emendation—can be adduced the fact that in some MSS and VSS (614 ae; syr. copt. h [plur.] boh.) 'glory' appears before 'Lord' " (cited in Adamson, p. 104 n. 10).

25. Ropes, p. 187; Dibelius, p. 128; Davids, *Epistle*, pp. 106–7.

26. Ropes, p. 187, calls it a genitive of characteristic, limiting the whole preceding phrase: *tou kuriou . . . Christou*. Bo Reicke, *Epistles*, p. 27 and p. 65n. 13, also interprets it as a qualitative genitive, *not* referring to *tou kuriou hēmōn*, but rather to the preceding *pistis*, for *kuriou* is already determined by *hēmōn*. He therefore translates it, "the glorious faith in our Lord Jesus Christ."

27. Adamson, p. 103.

28. Mayor, p. 78; cf. Nicoll, 4:435. Sidebottom, p. 38; Adamson, p. 104, etc., who follow him. Sophie Laws, *A Commentary on the Epistle of James* (San Francisco: Harper and Row, 1980), pp. 95–97, however, questions this interpretation and suggests that James's use of *doxa* reflects an understanding of Jesus as " 'theophany', a manifestation of the presence of God" (p. 97).

29. Hort, pp. 47–48, notes that "the faith of Christ as the glory was peculiarly at variance with this favoritism shown to the rich: since He who represented the very majesty of heaven was distinguished by His lowliness and poverty. . . . Here [James] rebukes the contemptuous usage of poor men even such as the Incarnate Glory of God Himself became"; cf. G. R. Beasley-Murray, *The General Epistles: James, 1 Peter, Jude and 2 Peter,* Bible Guides (New York: Abingdon, 1969), p. 27. See also Ronald Ward, "James," in *The New Bible Commentary Revised* (London: Inter-Varsity, 1970), p. 1227.

30. E.g., Bernard Weiss, *A Commentary on the New Testament* (New York: Funk and Wagnalls, 1906), 4:241; cf. William Barclay, *The Letters of James and Peter* (Philadelphia: Westminster, 1976), p. 65; A. E. Barnett, "Letter of James," in *The Interpreter's Dictionary of the Bible* (Nashville: Abingdon, 1962), 2: 797.

31. For an example of the proponents of the position that the incident was hypothetical, see Cain H. Felder, "Partiality and God's Law: An Exegesis of James 2:1–13," *Journal of Religious Thought* 39 (1982–83): 51–69. For a proponent of the view that the example is characteristic of the diatribe, see Thomas Leahy, "The Epistle of James," in *The Jerome Biblical Commentary* (Englewood Cliffs, N.J.: Prentice-Hall, 1968), pp. 369–77; cf. Songer, "James," pp. 114–15.

32. Dibelius, p. 129. He further notes that the parables of Jesus "contain stylizing elements similar to those which we surmise in James"; e.g., the unrealistic description of the unjust judge in Luke 18:4–5 can be compared with the unrealistic description in James 2:3 (p. 130).

33. Roy Bowen Ward, "Partiality in the Assembly: Jas. 2:2–4," *Harvard Theological Review* 62 (1969): 88; cf. Laws, pp. 7, 98; Arthur Cadoux, *The Thought of St. James* (London: James Clarke, 1944), p. 48, notes that the thought of James is "close to experience" and is "sparing of abstracts."

34. Cf. Davids, *Epistle*, p. 107.

35. Ward, "Partiality," p. 87; cf. Sidebottom, p. 38.

36. R. J. Knowling, *The Epistle of James* (London: Methuen, 1922), p. 41, notes that it is significant that this is the only place in the NT in which the word is used rather than the word "church" for assemblies—thus an inference for an early date and Palestinian setting. Cf. Robertson, *Word Pictures,* 6:28, Adamson, p. 105.

37. L. Rost, "Archäologische Bemerkungen zu einer Stelle des Jakobusbriefes (Jab. 2, 2f.)," *Palästinajahrbuch* 29 (1933): 53–66, cited in Dibelius, p. 131, n 43.

38. Dibelius, p. 131n. 43; cf. Wolfgang Schrage, *"sunagōge,* etc.," *Theological Dictionary of the New Testament* (Grand Rapids: Eerdmans, 1964–76), 7:838n. 256.

39. Debelius, p. 134; cf. Ropes, p. 189, who states that due to the widespread occasional use of *sunagōge,* no trustworthy place of writing can be determined; see also Sidebottom, p. 38.

40. E.g., Frank Stagg, "Exegetical Themes in James 1 and 2," *Review and Expositor* 66 (1969): 400.

41. Cf. Schrage, pp. 802–3.

42. See Hort, p. 49, who agrees. Dibelius agrees that in the LXX the words have the connotation which we described above. However, he claims that in later Judaism *ekklēsia* was used frequently for "the ideal community," while *sunagōge* often denoted "the empirical community" (pp. 133, 134). One, however, might be hard pressed to demonstrate that James is primarily making that distinction in his document. I. J. Peritz, "Synagogue," *Encyclopaedia Biblica: A Critical Dictionary of the Literary, Political and Religious History, the Archaeology, Geography and Natural History of the Bible* (1904), 4:4833, compares the terms in 2:2 with *episunagōge* in Heb. 10:25, and therefore feels that the translation "assembly" would be quite fitting.

43. Schrage, p. 838.

44. Plummer, p. 118; Joseph B. Mayor, *The Epistle of St. James,* 2nd ed. (Grand Rapids, Mich.: Baker, 1978), p. 80; Knowling, p.42.

45. James Moffatt, *The General Epistles: James, Peter, and Judas* (New York: Harper and Row, n.d.), p. 32.

46. Cf. Adamson, p. 105. Quite speculative is Beasley-Murray's suggestion that wealthy oppressors of the poor would hardly attend a Christian meeting (pp. 26–27). So also is Easton's surmise that because there were many rich Jews the discrimination would occur far more often in Judaism than in Christianity. He further states that these wealthy Jews "when traveling, would visit the local synagogues, where their expensive garments would secure them a warm welcome" (p. 36). In both commentaries a false distinction between Christian and Jewish assemblies is made, and thus, the conjectures arise.

47. Ropes, p. 190, does not feel that the traditional meaning of *kalōs*—"in a good seat," "comfortable"—is justified here. Rather, "some polite idiom in the sense of 'please,' 'pray,' is to be suspected," he states. It would seem, however, that the contrast with the latter part of the phrase might lend weight to the traditional translation.

48. Ibid.

49. Plumptre, p. 64.

50. Theodor H. Gaster, *The Dead Sea Scriptures* (Garden City, N.Y.: Doubleday, 1956), p. 16; cf. p. 18 in the 2nd ed.

51. F. C. Cook, ed., *The Holy Bible, with an Explanatory and Critical Commentary,* 12 vols. (London: John Murray, 1881) 12:123–24, notes this usage (and appeals to 1 Cor. 6 as evidence for it) but disagrees that such is the usage here.

52. Josephus *Life* 54. The word use here is not *sunagōge* but *proseuchē,* which literally means "place of prayer." However, some contend that it is another word for synagogue—e.g., W. Bacher, "synagogue," *A Dictionary of the Bible, Dealing with Its Language, Literature and Contents, Including the Biblical Theology*, ed., James Hastings (New York: Charles Scribner's Sons, 1911), 4:642, and a foot note in the Loeb Classical Library translation of *Life,* p. 103 (the latter's reference to Acts 16:13, 16, seems to contradict this view, seeing as only a small group of women were

at the meeting place at Philippi—and at least ten men are needed for a synagogue worship). It is possible that this great *proseuchē,* which was in the city, was used as a synagogue; see footnote in William Whiston's translation of *Life* (Grand Rapids, Mich.: Kregel, 1960), p. 14.

53. B. Talmud *Kethuboth* 5a. A note in the Talmud indicates that the phrase "public affairs" literally means "affairs of many" (B. Talmud, ed. I. Epstein, 35 vols. [London: Soncino Press, 1948–52], 17:14n.4).

54. See *De Vet Syn.* 1.3, p.l., c.11, cited in Adam Clarke, *Clarke's Commentary* (New York: Abingdon-Cokesbury, 1938), 6:809.

55. Clarke, *Commentary,* 6:809.

56. Ward, "Communal Concern" and "Partiality," pp. 87–97; Plummer, pp. 126–27, who also notes that Jewish courts were frequently held in the synagogues.

57. Cook, pp. 123–24. While Davids, *Epistle,* p. 109, correctly recognizes that a judicial setting is portrayed in James, the *Sitz im Leben* of a Christian church-court, which he argues for, seems incorrect. What would strangers be doing in a Christian *beth-din* patterned after the inferred one of 1 Cor. 6:1–11?

58. B. Talmud *Yebamoth* 65b.

59. J. Talmud *Sanhedrin* 1:1.

60. Mishnah *Sanhedrin* 1:1; 3:1.

61. B. Talmud *Baba Kamma* 80a; see also J. Talmud Sanhedrin 1:1.

62. See Ramsey MacMullen, *Roman Social Relations, 50 B.C. to A.D. 284* (New Haven: Yale Univ. Press, 1974), pp. 39–40.

63. B. Talmud *Shebu'oth* 31a. The footnote by the Talmud editors explains: "In order that the judges be not biased in your favour, and the poorly dressed man be not intimidated."

64. Ibid., 30b.

65. Ward, "Communal Concern," p. 92; idem, "Partiality," p. 92.

66. Dibelius, p. 135.

67. Ward, "Partiality," p. 94; cf. "Communal Concern," p. 99–107. Ward, however, feels that the other well-dressed man is also a member. He bases his argument on what he calls "a curious feature of the example": the person in fine clothes is never called *plousios;* thus the antithesis is not between "rich and poor," but between " 'a man with gold rings' and 'poor'!" ("Communal Concern," p 106); see also p. 98; "Partiality," p. 96; and Davids, *Epistles,* p. 108, who takes this stance.

For more debate on the question of "member or nonmember," "Christian or non-Christian," see Adamson, p. 30, who though not agreeing with Ward's judicial interpretation, agrees that the rich and poor incomers *may* be Christians, but only visitors. There is, however, strong opposition to this stance. Ropes, p. 191, agrees that they are visitors, distinguished from the congregation, but "nothing indicates, or suggests, that they are members of sister churches. They are undoubtedly outsiders, whether Jews or Gentiles." Cf. also Knowling, pp. 43, 47, who contends that they are rich Jews. Had they been members of the church they would have had their places and there would be no need for places to be assigned to them; cf. Elliot-Binns, "James," p. 1023. Zahn, p. 299, argues that James is depicting a scene where pagans may visit a Christian meeting. At the same time there are those who feel that it is not necessary to decide whether the rich person (or even the poor one) is supposed to be a Christian. See Cook, p., 123. Plummer, p. 126, indicates that the wealthy should not be thought of as exclusively or principally Christians. He, however, goes on to suggest that the rich in these verses are principally Sadducees. It seems obvious to us that the problem with the debate is an obsession with an issue which is not the concern of the author. Nowhere in the passage do we find any interest in "Christian versus non-Christian," "member versus nonmember."

68. Bo Reicke, *Diakonie, Festfreude und Zelos: In Verbindung mit der Altchrist-lichen Agapenfeir* (Uppsala: A. B. Lundequistska Bokhandeen, 1951), pp. 342–44; idem, *The Epistles of James, Peter, and Jude* (New York: Doubleday, 1964), p. 27. We must note that Reicke's argument is based on the presupposition that the document is late and represents a Roman social setting. See Cook, p. 123, who suggests also that a gold ring worn by a Roman "might be the simple badge of the wearer's rank."

69. Juvenal *Satire* 1.25–30 (trans. Ramsay, LCL).

70. Martial *Epigrams* 11.59 (trans. Page, LCL).

71. Epictetus *Discourses* 1.22 (trans. Oldfather, LCL).

72. E. A. Judge, *The Social Pattern of the Christian Groups in the First Century* (London: Tyndale, 1960), p. 53.

73. Ibid.

74. Ropes, p. 189, notes that although *lampros* seems here to refer to elegant, luxurious, and fine clothing (cf. Rev. 18:14), the term is also used of freshness or cleanness (Rev. 15:6) and has nothing to do with costliness in that context; some-times it also appears to mean "shining" (Acts 10:30). Cf. Kenneth G. Phifer, "James 2:1–5," *Interpretation* 35 (1982):280, who notes that in Rev. 22:1 the same word is used to describe the brilliant river flowing from God's throne. Phifer suggests that the rich person is "brilliantly clothed, shining and effulgent." In constrast, the poor person has *ruparos* ("shabby") clothing. This word indicates "filthiness" and "dirti-ness" (cf. Rev. 22:11). The contrast James is drawing is between an impeccably dressed person and a filthy, smelly, poor individual.

75. See Luke 15:22; cf. Plumptre, p. 64; Ward, "Communal Concern" p. 82n. 8.

76. Shirley Jackson Case, *The Social Triumph of the Ancient Church* (London: George Allen and Unwin, 1934), p. 49.

77. Joachim Jeremias, *Jerusalem in the Time of Jesus* (Philadelphia: Fortress, 1969), p. 92.

78. *Diekrithēte* ("distinction") is the aorist passive of *diakrinō*. Bauer, p. 185, and Ropes, p. 192, have argued that the word used in the aorist passive has the meaning of "doubted, wavered." In the active voice, on the other hand, it has the meaning "to make a distinction, differentiate." Interestingly, however, Bauer's lexicon has shown that in the present passive infinitive *diakrinesthai tinos,* in Diognetus 5:1, should be translated "be differentiated from someone." It therefore seems that in view of the fact that the context of our passage gives this meaning, we should give the word this nuance here.

79. Ward, "Communal Concern," p. 95.

80. Easton, p. 38.

81. Dibelius, p. 138.

82. Ropes, p. 193.

83. Dibelius, p. 138; cf. Hort, p. 51, who suggests it might be taken as "in relation to the world," but probably, "in the eyes of the world." Ropes, p. 193, suggests a third possibility, viz., a dative of reference, or "interest." The phrase would therefore be translated "the poor by the standard of the world."

84. Dibelius, p. 137, notes that "the pride of the Poor which surfaces in 2:5 is not to be understood upon the basis of proletarian motives, but rather upon the basis of pietistic and eschatological motives." But we have argued above, and it is stated further by C. E. B. Cranfield, "The Message of James," *Scottish Journal of Theology* 18 (1965): 191, that there is no need to see in these verses an *Armenfröm-migkeit.*

85. Moule, *An Idiom Book,* p. 46; cf. Sidebottom, p. 40, who sees this phrase in James as referring to the literal poor. Interestingly, Laws, p. 103, suggests that "James

seems to take a middle course between the Matthean and Lucan versions of Jesus' promise of the kingdom to the poor. He neither spiritualizes the idea of poverty as Matthew does . . . for his poverty is literal poverty, nor does he show poverty as rewarded *per se,* as Luke appears to do."

86. Here we agree with Dibelius, p. 138, and Ropes, p. 194, that *plousious en pistei* refers to the sphere of faith.

87. Cf. Ropes, p. 194, who notes that the term here "denotes the great blessing which God offers to his chosen, being thus practically equivalent to salvation."

88. Ropes, pp. 193–94; cf. Cranfield, p. 191.

89. Stagg, "Exegetical Themes," p. 394 (emphasis added).

90. Ibid.

91. Dibelius, p. 138.

92. See Amos 8:4 (oppression of the poor); Jer. 7:6 (oppression of the stranger, orphan, widow); Ezek. 18:12 (oppression of poor and needy); cf. Wis. 2:10 (oppression of the righteous poor). Ropes, p. 196, states that if religious persecution was intended, *diōkousin* would be used rather than this term. We should note, in passing, that the fact that the pronoun *humōn* ("you") is used indicates that the readers ranked with the poor; cf. Leahy, p. 372; Sidebottom, p. 41.

93. Cf. Bauer, p. 410; Adamson, p. 110; Alexander Ross, *The Epistles of James and John,* a vol. of *The New International Commentary on the New Testament* (Grand Rapids, Mich.: Eerdman, 1954), p. 47 n.6.

94. Cf. Joseph Chaine, *L'Épître du Saint Jacques* (Paris: Librairie Lecoffre, 1927); Moffat, p. 33; Ropes, p. 196.

95. Paul H. Furfey, *"Plousios* and Cognates in the New Testament," *The Catholic Biblical Quarterly* 5 (1943): 251.

96. Bauer, p. 294.

97. Massey Shepherd, "The Epistle of James and the Gospel of Matthew," *Journal of Biblical Literature* 75 (1956): 51, notes that the phrase possibly alludes to baptism, as in Hermas *Similitude* 8.6 (cf. Laws, p. 105). However, he does state that "the phrase in James may be only a general description of the people of God, derived from Jewish usage."

98. Dibelius, p. 141.

99. So Hort, p. 53; Dibelius, pp. 141–42; Adamson, p. 113; see the latter two works for summaries and criticism of alternative "concessive" or "adversative" interpretation—that is, interpreting the particle as meaning "however."

100. Hort, p. 53.

101. Dibelius, p. 142, notes that the commandment here under discussion is the commandment of love from Lev. 19:18 (LXX); cf. Laws, pp. 107–9; and Felder, "Partiality and God's Law," pp. 60–61. Ward, "Communal Concern," pp. 25–26, however, questions to what extent James is directly dependent on the LXX translation of Leviticus. He asks, "Is the juxtaposition of partiality and the love-command due to the author's use of the text in Lev. 19, or is the presence of these two themes to be explained in some other way? The most that can be said at this point is . . . that it is not at all clear that the author is working with the LXX text here or elsewhere in the document."

102. Cf. Elliot-Binns, "James," p. 1023; Ropes, p. 197.

103. Dibelius, p. 144; he further suggests that the phrase *hupo tou nomou* means the "whole law."

104. Davids, *Epistle,* p. 119.

105. We should note here that it is within the context of James's concern for the poor that he discusses his doctrine of "justification by works." It is, however, outside the scope of this book to enter into a discussion of faith and works in James and

Paul. Suffice it to say that each man is dealing with a different concern—Paul with legalistic compliance to the law, and James with the ethical issue of one's attitude to the poor. As Peter Davids notes, for James "real faith is single-minded commitment to God, which then copies God in his care for the poor and oppressed" ("God and Mammon," *Sojourners* [March 1978], p. 28). The language of James and Paul also differs; e.g., *erga* in Paul must be understood in the context of the phrase *ta erga nomou* ("the works of law"), i.e., righteousness being obtained by one's personal nomistic service. On the other hand, *erga* for James is how one treats the poor—the one who is "ill-clad and in lack of daily food" (2:15). Cf. Joachim Jeremias, "Paul and James," *Expository Times* 66 (1954–55): 368–71; Stagg, "Exegetical Themes," p. 401; John A. T. Robinson, *Redating the New Testament* (Philadelphia: Westminster, 1976), pp. 126–28; T. B. Maston, "Ethical Dimensions of James," *Southwestern Journal of Theology* 12 (1969): 29–30; Sidebottom, pp. 16–18, 21; also Arthur E. Travis, "James and Paul: A Comparative Study," *Southwestern Journal of Theology* 12 (1969): 57–70, whose stated purpose is to demonstate that if the idea of faith and works is rightly understood, James and Paul are seen in perfect agreement. Karl Kautsky, *Foundations of Christianity* (New York: S. A. Russell, 1953), p. 362, gives an interesting twist to the pericope by suggesting that in these verses James "turns against the tendency to require the rich only to accept the creed in theory and not give up their money."

CHAPTER 5

1. W. Robertson Nicoll, *The Expositor's Greek Testament,* 5 vols. (Grand Rapids, Mich.: Eerdmans, 1956), 4:462.

2. See Bent Noack, "Jakobus wider die Reichen," *Studia Theologia* 18 (1964): 12; cf. Harold S. Songer, "James," in *The Broadman Bible Commentary,* 12 vols. (Nashville: Broadman, 1972), 12:130, who states that they are somewhat related.

3. F. C. Cook, ed., *The Holy Bible, with an Explanatory and Critical Commentary*, 12 vols. (London: John Murray, 1881), 12:139.

4. See R. J. Knowling, *The Epistle of James* (London: Methuen, 1922), p. 108.

5. See Thomas W. Leahy, "The Epistle of James," in *The Jerome Biblical Commentary* (Englewood Cliffs, N.J.: Prentice-Hall, 1968) p. 375, who notes also that the use of the direct address throughout indicates that the sections are parallel; also Ronald A. Knox, *A New Testament Commentary for English Readers* (New York: Sheed & Ward, 1956), 3:107; and Martin Dibelius, *James* (Philadelphia: Fortress, 1976), p. 230, who, however, does find problems which make the unity of the passages not readily apparant.

6. Noack, p. 13.

7. Cf. Paul H. Furfey, *"Plousios* and Cognates in the New Testament," *The Catholic Biblical Quarterly* 5 (1943): 248–51.

8. See Songer, "James," p. 130; Dibelius, p. 230.

9. Burton Scott Easton, "The Epistle of James," in *The Interpreter's Bible* 12 vols. (New York: Abingdon, 1957), 12:59.

10. Joseph B. Mayor, *The Epistle of James,* 2nd ed. (Grand Rapids, Mich.: Baker, 1978), p. 144. Sophie Laws, *A Commentary on the Epistle of James* (San Francisco: Harper & Row, 1980), p. 189, sees the connection with the immediately preceding verses being that 4:13–17 depicts "a second instance of human arrogance."

11. James Hardy Ropes, *A Critical and Exegetical Commentary on the Epistle of St. James* (New York: Charles Scribner's Sons, 1916), p. 276; cf. James Adamson, *The Epistle of James* (Grand Rapids, Mich.: Eerdmans, 1976), p. 183.

12. Songer, "James," p. 130.

13. Ibid., pp. 130–31.
14. Bo Reicke, *The Epistles of James, Peter, and Jude* (New York: Doubleday, 1964), p. 48; cf. Dibelius, p. 231. We must note that other scholars agree with Songer that this is just a friendly address, and that the author is not at all condemning the rich's trading. E. C. Blackman, *The Epistle of James* (London: SCM, 1957), p. 137, for example, sees the passage as dealing with the "industrious trader, who is prepared to experiment, and even make long journeys in the course of business," and his only mistake is that he is "too busy to have time for religion." See also Theodor Zahn, "Die Sociale Frage und die Innere Mission Nach dem Brief des Jakobus," *Zeitschrift für Kirchliche Wissenschaft und Kirchliches Leben* 10 (1889): 300, who is against any attempt at making James interested in any social question. He, therefore, contends that James does not suggest a change in social conditions—he is angry with profit-minded merchants, but he does not counsel them to change their jobs. Zahn states that James's emphasis is on the fact that they make their profits without God. See also Nicoll, 4:464, who sees the addressee as only erring through thoughtlessness.
15. Ronald Knox, p 107.
16. Adamson, p 178.
17. Reicke, *Epistles,* p. 48.
18. Knowling, p. 108.
19. Noack, p. 14; cf. A. T. Robertson, *Word Pictures in the New Testament,* 6 vols. (Nashville: Broadman, 1930–33) 6:55, who suggests that *emporeusometha* presents a vivid picture of the Jewish merchant of the time. See also Adolf Schlatter, *Der Brief des Jakobus* (Stuttgart: Calwer, 1956), p. 262; Nicoll, 4:462–63; Laws, pp. 189–90.
20. Alexander Ross, *The Epistles of James and John* (Grand Rapids, Mich.: Eerdmans, 1954), p. 82n. 6.
21. Adamson, p. 179.
22. Mikhail Rostovtzeff, *The Social and Economic History of the Hellenistic World,* 3 vols. (Oxford, Eng.: Clarendon, 1941), 2:1040–41.
23. Ibid., pp. 1041–43.
24. *Greek Anthology* 9.449 (trans. Paton, LCL)
25. Rostovtzeff, *The Hellenistic World,* 2:1045
26. M. P. Charlesworth, *Trade-Routes and Commerce of the Roman Empire* (Cambridge, Eng.: Cambridge University Press, 1926), p. 40.
27. William White, Jr., "Finances," in *The Catacombs and the Colosseum* (Valley Forge, Pa.: Judson, 1971), p. 230.
28. Lionel Casson, *Travel in the Ancient World* (London: George Allen & Unwin, 1974), p. 122.
29. Mikhail Rostovtzeff, *The Social and Economic History of the Roman Empire,* 2 vols. (Oxford, Eng.: Clarendon, 1957), 1:66; cf. Casson, p. 112.
30. Ibid.
31. See William M. Ramsay, "Roads and Travel (in NT)," *A Dictionary of the Bible, Dealing with Its Language, Literature and Contents, Including the Biblical Theology* (1912), supp. vol.: 387.
32. See Rostovtzeff, *The Roman Empire,* 1:66 F. M. Heichelheim, "Roman Syria," in *An Economic Survey of Ancient Rome,* 6 vols. (Baltimore: Johns Hopkins, 1933–40), 4:199–200.
33. We must note here that Syria and Palestine were regarded as a unit by such geographers as Strabo (*Geography* 16.2 1-2 [trans. Jones LCL]). We should also remember that the whole of that region of the Near East was interdependent economically, and commercial characteristics overlapped (see Joachim Jeremias, *Jerusalem in the Time of Jesus* [Philadelphia: Fortress, 1969], p. 27; Heichelheim,

p. 123). In our discussion, however; we deal with the geographical areas separately, e.g., Syria apart from Judea and Jerusalem, etc.

34. Charlesworth, p. 54.

35. Ibid., pp. 37–38.

36. See ibid., p. 42.

37. Ibid., p. 46.

38. Ibid.

39. Rostovtzeff, *The Roman Empire,* 1:266.

40. Chrysostom *Homilies on the Gospel of St. Matthew* 66:3.

41. Ibid., 63:4.

42. See Frederick C. Grant, *The Economic Background of the Gospels* (New York: Russell and Russell, 1973), p. 72.

43. We note here with Karl Kautsky, *Foundations of Christianity* (New York: S. A. Russell, 1953), p. 65, that "commerce and transportation were not distinct in those days. The merchant . . . had to bring the goods to market himself."

44. Rostovtzeff, *The Roman Empire,* 1:270.

45. Josephus *Against Apion* 1.12 (trans. Thackeray, LCL).

46. Arcadius Kahn, "Economic History," *Encyclopedia Judaica* (1971), 16:1274; cf. Salo W. Baron, *A Social and Religious History of the Jews,* 2 vols. (New York: Columbia University Press, 1951), 1:256 and 407n. 8.

47. Joseph Klausner, *Jesus of Nazareth* (New York: MacMillan, 1929), pp. 186–88; cf. Aristeas *The Letter of Aristeas* 114 (trans. Thackery, S.P.C.K.), who states that "the country is well adapted for commerce as well as for cultivation, and the city is rich in the arts and lacks none of the merchandise that is brought across the sea. It possesses havens well situated which supply its needs, that at Ascalon, and Joppa, and Gaza, as well as Ptolemais."

48. We must note that Josephus is here engaged in apologetics. Henry Daniel-Rops, *Daily Life in Palestine at the Time of Christ* (London: Weidenfeld and Nicolson, 1962), p. 246, suggests that the underlying purpose of Josephus's words may have been "to counter one of the antisemitical arguments of his day." Cf. Geoffrey A. Williamson, *The World of Josephus* (Boston: Little, Brown, and Co., 1964), chap. 18, "The Apologist," and passim.

49. Josephus *Antiquities* 13.10.6.

50. Cf. Marcus Jastrow, *A Dictionary of the Targumin, the Talmud Babli and Yerushalmi, and the Midrashic Literature,* 2 vols. (New York: Title, 1943), 1: 386–87.

51. J. Talmud *Yoma* 5:2. Emphasis added. The high priest also prays for "a year of cloddy earth [in consequence of ample rain (Jastrow, 1:274)] and dew, and moist, and ease. . . . Do not listen to the prayers of those who go on their way." It would seem that "those who go on their way" here are not the same persons who would be involved in the trade and commerce for which he prayed earlier; these are probably tourists or persons undertaking a mission other than a commercial one.

52. See, e.g., B. Talmud *Kethuboth* 112a; Josephus *Wars* 3.3.4; Aristeas *The Letter of Aristeas* 112; cf. Baron, 1:251; Klausner, p. 175.

53. See Pliny *Natural History* 13.9 (trans. Rackham, LCL); B. Talmud *Kethuboth* 112a; Strabo *Geography* 13.1.51.

54. Pliny *Natural History* 35.51; Strabo *Geography* 16.2.42, 45.

55. Jeremias, *Jerusalem,* pp. 27–57.

56. Ibid., p. 71.

57. Ibid., p. 28.

58. Ibid., pp. 31, 49.

59. See my Andrews University Th.D. dissertation (1981), "Poor and Rich in the

Epistle of James: A Socio-Historical and Exegetical Study," pp. 193–218, for a more detailed investigation.

60. Sir. 11:19.

61. 1 Enoch 97:8–10.

62. Seneca *Epistles* 101 (trans. Gummere, LCL).

63. Ibid.; cf. Pseudo-Phocylides 116f.: "No one knows what will happen the day after tomorrow, or even an hour from now, for trouble has no regard for mortals and the future is uncertain" (trans. and cited by Dibelius, p. 232). Philo also illustrates the uncertainty of plans when he speaks of the farmer who says: " 'I will sow, I will plant, the plants will grow, seeds and plant will yield crops, not only useful as affording food that we cannot do without, but so abundant as to give us enough and to spare.' Then all of a sudden a fire, or a storm, or persistent rain spoils everything. Sometimes all that he had reckoned on comes to pass, but the reckoner dies first without having had the benefits of them, and his expectations of enjoying the fruits of his toil proves a vain one" *(Allegorical Interpretation of Genesis II, III* 3.80 [trans. Colson and Whitaker, LCL].

64. Ropes, p 280, notes that *kauchasthe* is thrown into strong emphasis by *age nun*.

65. Mayor, p. 147.

66. Easton, p. 61; cf. Dibelius, p. 231, who contends that there is not even a superficial link between this verse and the context; Dibelius finds it difficult to comprehend the writer's reason for inserting the verse and writes of it: "It stands isolated between two related texts."

67. Reicke, *Epistles,* p. 49, suggests that the verse "apparently contains a traditional maxim regarding sins of omission, which the author quotes to give emphasis to his admonitions."

CHAPTER 6

1. Cf. R. J. Knowling, *The Epistle of James* (London: Methuen, 1922), p. 114; L.E. Elliot-Binns, "James," in *Peake's Commentary* (Hong Kong: Thomas Nelson and Sons, 1962), p. 1024.

2. James Hardy Ropes, *A Critical and Exegetical Commentary on the Epistle of St. James* (New York: Charles Scribner's Sons, 1916), p. 276.

3. See James B. Adamson, *The Epistle of James* (Grand Rapids, Mich.: Eerdmans, 1976), p. 12; Thomas W. Leahy, "The Epistle of James,"in *The Jerome Biblical Commentary* (Englewood Cliffs, N.J.: Prentice-Hall, 1968), p. 375; Ropes, pp. 282–83; Martin Dibelius, *James* (Philadelphia: Fortress, 1976), p. 231; Bo Reicke, *The Epistles of James, Peter, and Jude* (New York: Doubleday, 1964), p. 52; E. Malcolm Sidebottom, *James, Jude and 2 Peter* (Greenwood, S.C.: Attic, 1967), p. 56; Burton Scott Easton, "The Epistle of James," in *The Interpreter's Bible,* 12 vols. (New York: Abingdon, 1957), 12:62.

4. J. P. Lange and J. J. Van Oosterzee, *The Epistle General of James,* a vol. of *A Commentary on the Holy Scriptures: Critical, Doctrinal and Homiletical* (New York: Charles Scribner's Sons, 1915), pp. 127–33.

5. See R. C. H. Lenski, *The Interpretation of the Epistle to the Hebrews and the Epistle of James* (Columbus, Ohio: Wartburg, 1946), p. 45; Adamson, p. 184; cf. Paul H. Furfey, *"Plousios* and Cognates in the New Testament," *The Catholic Biblical Quarterly* 5 (1943):243.

6. Robert G. Bratcher, "Exegetical Themes in James 3–5," *Review and Expositor* 66 (1969): 410n.17; cf. E. H. Plumptre, ed., *The General Epistle of St. James* (Cambridge, Eng.: The University Press, 1915), p. 96.

7. Others have schematized James's concerns differently. James Moffatt, *The*

General Epistles of James, Peter, and Jude (New York: Harper and Row. n.d.), pp. 68–70, sees three charges being brought against the rich here: (1) v. 3b, the rapacity of the wealthy in hoarding their money; (2) v. 4, fraudulent treatment of their farm laborers; and (3) vv.5–6, wanton luxury with its social cruelty. Joseph B. Mayor, *The Epistle of James,* 2nd ed. (Grand Rapids, Mich.: Baker 1978), p. 154, sees James emphasizing the sin and the folly of the rich: "The rich are represented as sinning (1) in getting their wealth by injustice, (2) in spending it merely on their own pleasures. Their folly is shown (1) in laying up their treasures on earth, (2) especially in doing so in the very day of judgement"; cf. Richard L. Scheef, Jr., "The Letter of James," in *The Interpreter's One-Volume Commentary on the Bible* (Nashville: Abingdon, 1971), p. 922. A twofold division as I have presented above seems, however, more in line with the passage: vv. 2–3 and 5 illustrating the motif of luxurious living, while vv. 4 and 6 specifically emphasize the rich's oppression of the poor.

8. Testament of Issachar 4:2.

9. Easton, p. 64.

10. Horace *Epistles* 1.6 (trans. Fairclough, LCL).

11. Henry B. Tristram, *The Natural History of the Bible: Being a Review of the Physical Geography, Geology, and Meteorology of the Holy Land; with a Description of Every Animal and Plant Mentioned in Holy Scriptures* (London: S.P.C.K., 1880), p. 326.

12. F. C. Cook, ed., *The Holy Bible, with an Explanatory and Critical Commentary,* 12 vols (London: John Murray, 1881), 12:143.

13. See Easton, p. 65.

14. See Dibelius, p. 236.

15. R. A. Martin, *James* (Minneapolis: Augsburg, 1982), p. 45, does note that the Greek preposition *en,* which is translated "for" in the phrase *"for* the last days" (5:3 RSV), can be translated "in." Thus the phrase can be translated as "*in* the last days," and this latter translation would lend credence to the notion that for James the last days had already begun. Although we must not ignore this as a possibility, the whole sense of the passage seems to point to the future. As to the language used to describe the riches, Mayor, p. 149, interestingly notes that the terms chosen indicate and refer to types of wealth: *sesēpe,* to corn and other perishable products of the earth; *sētobrōta,* to rich fabrics; and *iōtai,* to metals. Dibelius, p. 236, disagrees with this interpretation of *sesēpe* and argues for a metaphorical one. His argument, however, is not convincing. Rather James's concern with agriculture lends credence to Mayor's suggestion. Cf. Sophie Laws, *A Commentary on the Epistle of James* (San Francisco: Harper and Row, 1980), p. 198, who also demurs to Mayor's suggestion.

16. Franz Mussner, *Der Jakobusbrief* (Freiberg: Herder, 1967), p. 194, suggests that the rust attests to some extent to the social injustice by the rich that results in the need to cry to heaven. Furthermore, he notes that instead of using their wealth to help the poor in their needs, the rich accumulated it and allowed it to rot. In this latter point he follows John Calvin, *Commentaries on the Catholic Epistles* (Grand Rapids: Eerdmans, 1948), p. 344, who feels that James is suggesting that the riches should be employed to meet basic human needs. See also Francis D. Nichol, ed., *Seventh-day Adventist Bible Commentary* (Washington, D.C.: Review and Herald, 1953–57), 7:537, which suggests that the riches "might have been used in service for God and man." Ropes, p. 285, however, finds these suggestions to be needless and far-fetched.

17. It is possible that this verse is an amplificaton of "you have laid up treasure" of v. 3b, as Dibelius, p. 238, has suggested.

18. Scheef, p. 922.

19. Adamson, p. 186.
20. Leslie C. Mitton, *The Epistle of James* (Grand Rapids, Mich.: Eerdmans, 1966), p. 180.
21. B. Talmud *Baba Metzia* 111a.
22. Sir. 34:22; cf. 1 Enoch 96:5.
23. See Luke 12:16; John 4:35.
24. See Ropes, p. 288.
25. Seneca *Epistles* 90.39. (trans. Gummere, LCL).
26. Ibid., p. 114; cf. W. E. Heitland, *Agricola* (Cambridge, Eng.: The University Press, 1921), pp. 246–48.
27. Ramsay MacMullen, *Roman Social Relations: 50 B.C. to A.D. 284* (New Haven: Yale University Press, 1974), p. 6; see pp. 6–14 and pp. 149–50nn. 25–27 for Latin evidences.
28. Frederick C. Grant, *The Economic Background of the Gospels* (New York: Russell and Russell, 1973), p. 66; cf. Knowling, p.121.
29. F. M. Heichelheim, "Roman Syria," in *An Economic Survey of Ancient Rome*, 6 vols. (Baltimore: John Hopkins, 1933–40), 4:146.
30. Josephus *Antiquities* 17.10.9; 17.11.2; 17.13.5; 18.1.1; *Wars* 2.5.1; cf. Joachim Jeremias, *Jerusalem in the Time of Jesus* (Philadelphia: Fortress, 1969), p. 92.
31. See Mishnah *Demai* 6:11; cf. *Hallah* 4:7, 11; see also Josephus *Life* 9.
32. Victor A. Tcherikover, Alexander Fuks, and Manahem Stern, eds., *Corpus Papyrorum Judaicarum*, (Cambridge, Mass.: Harvard University Press, 1964), 1:6. The editors of this collection of papyri feel that Jeddous, who drove off the collecting official, was an important rich landowner in the village; otherwise he would not dare to act as he did. Gerd Theissen, *Sociology of Early Palestinian Christianity* (Philadelphia: Fortress, 1977) p. 56, however, infers that he was a tenant on the landlord's estate. Cf. Matt. 21:33–45 and parallels.
33. Mishnah *Sanhedrin* 1:1; 3:1.
34. MacMullen, *Roman,* pp. 39–40; see B. Talmud *Baba Kamma* 80a for the case of Rabbi Ishmael's father who was a big property owner in Upper Galilee.
35. Jean Cantinat, *Les Épîtres de Saint Jacques et de Saint Jude* (Paris: Librarie Lecoffre, 1973), pp. 224–25; Mikhail Rostovtzeff, *The Social and Economic History of the Roman Empire*, 2 vols. (Oxford, Eng.: Clarendon, 1957), 1:270.
36. See Josephus *Life* 76.
37. Gerald Rendall, *The Epistle of James and Judaic Christianity* (Cambridge, Eng.: The Universilty Press, 1927). p. 32.
38. Louis Finkelstein, "The Pharisees: Their Origin and Their Philosophy," *Harvard Theological Review* 22 (1925): 189.
39. Josephus *Antiquities* 13.10.6.
40. B. Talmud *Yebamoth* 63a. That is if we take Eleazar's statement as referring to the landlord and not the laborer.
41. Heinz Kreissig, 'Die Landwirtschaftliche Situation in Palästina vor dem Judäischen Krieg," *Acta Antiqua* 17 (1969): 241–42.
42. See Karl Kautsky, *Foundations of Christianity* (New York: S. A. Russell, 1953), p. 65.
43. Kreissig, p. 242.
44. Ibid.
45. For some evidence in support of this see Louis Finkelstein, *Akiba: Scholar, Saint and Martyr* (New York: Atheneum, 1970), p. 17, and the letter to him from W. F. Albright on p. 320n. 16.
46. S. Applebaum, "Judaea as a Roman Province; the Countryside as a Political and Economic Factor," in *Aufstieg und Niedergang der Römischen Welt,* ed.

Hildegard Temporini and Wolfgang Haase (Berlin: Walter de Gruyter, 1922–79), 8:365; Louis Finkelstein, *The Pharisees: The Sociological Background of Their Faith,* 2 vols. (Philadelphia: The Jewish Publications Society of America, 1938), 1:38.

47. B. Talmud *Baba Bathra* 145b.

48. Kreissig, pp. 246–47.

49. Ibid., pp. 241, 247.

50. Ibid., p. 246.

51. Ibid., p. 247.

52. Mishnah *Shebiith* 10:4.

53. Ibid., 10:3.

54. B. Talmud *Gittim* 37a; cf. Aaron Rothkoff, "Prosbul," *Encyclopedia Judaica* (New York: MacMillan, 1971), 13:1181.

55. Josephus *Wars* 2.17.6 (trans. Whiston); cf. Applebaum, p. 370; also Kreissig, p. 243, who feels that the introduction of the prosbul was done at the initiative of the big landlords, in order that they could collect debts at any time. We should note that it seems most probably that the School of Hillel was more sensitive to the cause of the rich than the School of Shammai. This is evident in the Tractate *Peah;* e.g., it was reported that the School of Shammai said: "If produce is proclaimed 'ownerless' for the benefit of the poor it is deemed ownerless and tithe-free."But the School of Hillel taught: "It can only be deemed ownerless and tithe-free if it is proclaimed ownerless equally for the benefit of the rich, as in the year of Release" (Mishnah *Peah* 6:1).

56. See Joseph Klausner, *Jesus of Nazareth* (New York: MacMillan, 1929), p. 179; Kreissig, p. 246; Finkelstein, *Pharisees,* 1:38–39. Klausner further notes that in some cases the "children would be forced to become hirlings or laborers since the small-holding sufficed only for the oldest son who received 'a double share' of the inheritance. The other sons, not having land enough for their needs, were, in spite of themselves, turned into members of the 'proletariat,' the class which owns nothing but its powers of work."

57. Cf. Isa. 58:3; Jer. 22:13; Mal. 3:5; Tob. 4:14; Sir. 34:22.

58. See Mishnah *Baba Metzia* 9:11–12.

59. Klausner, pp. 180–81.

60. See my dissertation, p. 216n.7., for arguments for the existence of slaves in Palestine.

61. See Samuel Dickey, "Some Economic and Social Conditions of Asia Minor Affecting the Expansion of Christianity," in *Studies in Early Christianity,* ed. Shirley Jackson Case (New York: Century, 1928), pp. 403–5; Salo W. Baron, *A Social and Religious History of the Jews,* 2 vols. (New York: Columbia University Press, 1952), 1:207.

62. Kautsky, p. 47.

63. See Dickey, p. 402; cf. Mikhail Rostovtzeff, *The Social and Economic History of the Hellenistic World,* 3 vols. (Oxford, Eng.: Clarendon, 1941), 2:1126–27. It is interesting to note that even priests and levites were used as day laborers, and the landlords would pay for their work with gifts for the priests. Thus Kreissig is led to comment that instead of keeping the commandments of the Torah, the spirit of commerce and finance which Hellenism had brought into the oriental world had taken over even in Judea (p. 244).

64. Josephus *Wars* 2.13.6; cf. David M. Rhoads, *Israel in Revolution: 6–74 C. E.* (Philadephia: Fortress, 1976), pp. 47–93, esp. pp. 80–82; Klausner, pp. 182, 189; Applebaum, p. 380. On p. 385 Applebaum notes the close connection between the Jewish activist movement and the struggle for cultivatable land. It is a reflection, he suggests, on the problem of land shortage, exacerbated by heavy taxation and tenurial oppression. Cf. Morton Smith, "Zealots and Sicarii: Their Origins and

Relations," *Harvard Theological Review* 64 (1971): 1-19; and Appendix A. "The Zealots," in *The Beginning of Christianity, Part I: The Acts of the Apostles,* ed. F. J. Foakes Jackson and Kirsopp Lake (London: MacMillan, 1920). N. B., Applebaum contends that much of Smith's arguments is semantic; but see Rhoads, pp. 94-122, for a fairly precise use of party terms.

65. Ralph Martin, "The Life-Setting of the Epistle of James in the Light of Jewish History," in *Biblical and Near Eastern Studies,* ed. Gary Tuttle (Grand Rapids, Mich.: Eerdmans, 1978), pp. 97-103; for support of this suggestion he points to 1:20; 2:11-13; 3:13-18; 4:1-4.

66. Cir. 34:21-2.

67. Gerhard Kittel, "Der geschichtliche Ort des Jakobusbriefes," *Zeitschrift für die Neutestamentlich Wissenschaft* 41 (1942): 82.

68. See the Minor Tractates of the Talmud, *'Aboth De Rabbi Nathan* 32b.

69. Tom Hanks, "Why People Are Poor," *Sojourners* (Jan. 1981): 22.

70. See Adamson, p. 188; Moffatt, p. 71; Theodor Zahn, "Die Sociale Frage und die Innere Mission Nach dem Brief des Jakobus," *Zeitschrift für Kirchliche Wissenschaft un Kirchliches Leben* 10 (1889): 301. Debelius, p. 239; Sidebottom, p 58; Reicke, *Epistles,* p. 50; etc.

71. Luis Alonso Schökel, "James 5, 2 [sic] and 4, 6," *Biblica* 56 (1975): 73.

72. Mayor, p. 155, explains this change by suggesting that it makes it more vivid: "the present brings the action before our eyes and makes us dwell upon this, as the central point, in contrast with the accompanying circumstances." Mayor's argument is not persuasive, however.

73. Cf. A. Feuillet, "Le Sens du mot Parousie dans l'Evangile de Matthieu. Comparison entre Matth. XXIV et Jac. v. 1-11," in *The Background of the New Testament and Its Eschatology,* ed. W. D. Davis and D. Daube (Cambridge, Eng.: Cambridge University Press, 1956), p. 276n.1.

74. Schökel, "James 5, 2," p. 74. Those who see *dikaios* ("righteous one") as the implied subject and see the oppressed class as passive sufferers translate it as a passive statement. Ropes, however, treats it as a rhetorical question (with *dikaios* as the implied subject): "Does not he resist you?"—he understands the resistance as eschatological, i.e., at the Day of Judgment (p. 292). Schökel, as well as Feuillet, p. 276, by recognizing the relation with 4:6 and the fact that *Theos* is the subject, translates the sentence as rhetorical.

75. Ropes, p. 292, and Feuillet, p. 276, note that *antitassomai* expresses a hostile attitude, an active resistance; cf. Esther 3:4; Prov. 3:15 in the LXX.

76. Schökel, "James 5, 2." p. 74.

77. Moffatt, pp. 67-68; see Adamson, pp. 21, 184; Bratcher, p. 410; Kittel, 'Der geschichtliche Ort," p. 83.

78. See Philip Seidensticker, "St. Paul and Poverty," in *Gospel Poverty: Essays in Biblical Theology* (Chicago: Franciscan Herald, 1977), p. 102.

79. Feuillet, p. 279. Feuillet argues in his article that in James 5:1-11 and in Matt. 24 the Parousia of Christ is understood in the sense of the historic judgment of the Jewish people, and this is quite different from the other NT writings which see the Parousia as the supreme manifestation of Christ at the end of the history of the world (see esp. pp. 278-79). Cf. W. Robertson Nicoll, *The Expositors' Greek Testament* 5 vols. (Grand Rapids, Mich.: Eerdmans, 1956), 4:465-66; Martin Hengel, *Property and Riches in the Early Church* (Philadelphia: Fortress, 1974), pp. 17-18. Laws, p. 13n.1, however, finds Feuillet's argument unconvincing.

80. Cf. Jer. 25:34, which calls upon the "shepherds" to "wail and cry" for the day of slaughter; see also Ezek. 21:15; Isa. 34:2-4; Jer. 12:3.

81. 1 Enoch 94:6-99:15 (emphasis added).

Index

Compiled by James Sullivan

Acts of the Apostles, 35
Adamson, James B., 51–52, 104n.36, 116n.1, 117n.7, 119n.24, 121n.67, 123n.99
age nun, 68, 70, 81
agriculturalists, 30, 59, 64, 69, 70, 81–98, 107n.12; small farmers, as, 88. *See also* landlord ownership
'am ha-'aretz, 20, 30, 108n.29
'anah ('anaw), 25
anawin-piety, 40, 58, 63
'ani, 25, 40, 108n.3
apocryphal literature, 24, 28–29
Applebaum, 130–31n.64
Aristeas, 126n.47
authorship of James, 5–9, 103nn.29, 30
Barnett, A.E., 113n.5
Baron, Salo, 31
Bartlett, David, 101nn.11, 16, 113n.11
Bauer, Walter, 116nn.39, 48, 122n.78
Beasley-Murray, G.R., 120n.46
Beatitudes, 33, 38, 63
Berger, Klaus, 99n.1
Blackman, E.C., 125n.14
blasphemy, 64–67
Blondel, Jean-Luc, 112n.55

brother, 41, 43
Bruce, F.F., 119n.24
Chrysostum, 74
Clarke, Adam, 56
class. *See* social stratification
communism of early church, 35, 111n.50
Cook, F.C., 56
Cynics, 48,105n.47
dal, 25, 40
Davids, Peter, 11, 52, 102n.28, 110n.33, 111n.48, 116–17n.1, 119n.24, 124n.105
Dead Sea scrolls. *See* Essenes; Qumran
debt, 88–91, 130n.55. *See also* agriculturalists; landlord ownership
Diaspora, 9, 10, 24, 31, 77, 107n.19
Dibelius, Martin, 38, 39, 43, 46–47, 53, 58, 61, 63, 105n.47, 119n.32, 122n.84, 123nn. 99, 101, 103, 124n.5, 127n.66
Easton, Burton Scott, 42
'ebyon, 25
'edah, 54
Egypt, 16–18
ekklēsia, 54, 120n.42
Eleazar, Rabbi, 87, 129n.40

Elliot-Binns, L.E., 51, 121n.67
equestrian rule, 19, 60
eschatology. *See* intertestamental
    period; kingdom; Parousia
Essenes, 31–32
farmers. *See* agriculturalists
Feuillet, A., 103n.32, 131nn.75, 79
Finkelstein, Louis, 20, 107n.22,
    110n.24
Flusser, D., 33, 111n.40
Foakes Jackson, F.J., 9
Forbes, P.B.R., 119n.24
Form Criticism, 1, 11, 99n.1
Furfey, Paul, 64, 108n.3
Gager, John G., 19, 101n.16,
    112n.55
Gaster, Theodor H., 55, 103n.31,
    105n.45
George, Augustin, 109n.5
glory, 51–52
Gordis, Robert, 109n.10
Grant, Robert, 34, 37
Guthrie, Donald, 6, 102–3nn.21,
    28
Hanks, Tom, 93
Harrington, Daniel, 4, 100n.8
Hellenism, 14–17, 60, 71–72
Hengel, Martin, 15, 106n.2,
    111n.50, 131n.79
Hillel, 89, 130n.55
Hort, F.J., 39, 50–51, 113n.5,
    118n.18, 119n.29, 120n.42,
    122n.83
Howard, George, 118n.17
Hoyt, 109n.10
humiliation, 41–42, 44
intertestamental period, 24, 28–30,
    38; apocalyptic literature of,
    28–29, 38, 78, 95–97, 115n.35
Jeremias, Joachim, 76, 106n.2,
    111n.37
Jerusalem, 77, 96

Johanan, Rabbi, 56
Josephus, 31, 55–56, 75–76, 87,
    92, 126n.48
Judge, Edwin A., 102n.19,
    112n.53
judicial background, 57–61
Julianus of Egypt, 72
kalōs, 65, 120n.47
Karris, Robert, 32, 110n.34
Kautsky, Karl, 91, 124n.105,
    126n.43
Keck, Leander, 34, 113n.9
Kimbrough, Jr., S.T., 100n.5
kingdom, 33, 34, 35, 62, 123n.85.
    See also Parousia
Kittel, Gerhard, 8, 103n.32
Klausner, Joseph, 75, 91, 130n.56
Knowling, R.J., 119n.36, 121n.67
Kreissig, Heinz, 87, 130nn.55, 63
laborers. *See* agriculturalists; land-
    lord ownership; slavery
Lake, Kirsopp, 9
landlord ownership, 26, 30, 59, 64,
    85–91, 107n.12, 129n.32,
    130n.55; absentee, 87–91. *See
    also* agriculturalists
Laws, Sophie, 119n.28, 122–
    23nn.85, 124n.10
Leahy, Thomas W., 124n.5
loans. *See* debt
LXX. *See* Septuagint
MacMullen, Ramsay, 106n.2
Malherbe, Abraham, 2, 105n.47,
    108n.32
Malina, Bruce, 101nn.11, 14
Martin, Ralph, 92, 114–15,
    128n.15
Mayor, Joseph B., 114n.17,
    128n.7, 131n.72
Meeks, Wayne, 99n.1
merchants, 64, 68–80, 125n.19;
    travel of, 71–77

Milligan, G., 47
Mitton, C. Leslie, 84
Moffatt, J., 54, 127–28n.7
monarchial period, 24, 26–27
Morgenstern, Julian, 27
Moule, C. D. F., 62
Moulton, J. H., 47
Mussner, Franz, 113n.11, 128n.16
Neusener, Jacob, 106n.2
Nicoll, W. Robertson, 112n.1
Parousia, 37, 95, 103–4n.32,
   131n.79. *See also* kingdom
Pauline literature, 35–37
Pax Romana, 18
penēs, 108–9n.3
Phifer, Kenneth G., 122n.74
pietism, 31, 38–47, 59, 113n.9. *See
   also* spiritualizing
piety of *anawin,* 40, 58, 63
pistis, 50–51, 61, 117nn.6, 12,
   118n.17, 123n.86
plousios, 38–42, 68, 82, 109n.3,
   121n.67
Plummer, 114n.23, 121n.67
Plumtre, E. H. 113n.5
Polhill, J. B. 102n.20, 105n.47
poreia, 46–47
postexilic period, 24
premonarchial period, 24, 25–26
prosbul, promulgation of. *See*
   Hillel
Psalms, 24, 28, 29
ptōchos, 35, 58, 61, 62, 108nn.2, 3,
   111–12n.51
Qumran, 24, 32, 33, 62, 103n.31,
   105n.45, 111n.50
Randall, Gerald H., 102–3nn.28,
   29
rash'im, 28
Redaction Criticism, 1, 11, 99n.1
Reicke, Bo, 105n.48, 119n.26,
   122n.74, 127n.67

revolution. *See* violence
Riches, John K., 99n.2
Robertson, Archibald, 117n.7,
   125n.19
Robinson, John A. T., 102n.20,
   104n.35
Roman Empire, 14–23, 73–79
Ropes, James Hardy, 39, 41–43,
   46–47, 52, 105n.47, 115nn.31,
   32, 35, 116n.1, 119n.26,
   120nn.39, 47, 121n.67,
   122nn.74, 88, 123nn.87, 92,
   128n.16, 131nn.74, 75
Ross, Alexander, 71
Rostovtzeff, M., 74–75, 107n.12
rural–urban divisions, 22–23, 26
rush, 25
Sadducees, 20, 30, 76, 87, 92,
   121n.67
Sanhedrin, 20
sapiential writings, 24, 27–28, 30
Schlatter, Adolf, 10
Schökel, Luis Alonso, 94
Scroggs, Robin, 3, 99n.4, 101n.11,
   106n.2, 112n.54
Seneca, 78–79, 86
Septuagint, 46, 49, 54, 63, 108n.3,
   116n.39
Shammai, 64, 130n.55
Shepherd, Massey H., 102n.20
Sicarii, 92
Sidebottom, E. Malcolm, 101n.19,
   102–3nn.20, 28, 105nn.47, 50,
   116n.1, 122n.85
slavery, 16, 20, 91, 106n.2,
   107n.19, 130n.60
small farmers. *See* agriculturalists
social science models, 2, 3, 4, 5
social stratification, 5, 13–23, 26–
   27, 36–37, 110n.24
Songer, Harold, 70, 105n.47
spiritualizing: in James, 38–47, 53,

104n.36, 113-14n.12; in Scripture, 33, 110n.36, 123n.85. *See also* pietism
Stagg, Frank, 63
Stenzel, Meinrad, 40
Stoics, 105n.47
sun, 46, 116n.39
sunagōge/synagogue, 53-57, 120nn.39, 42, 120-21n.52
Synoptics, 32
Syria, 10, 17, 73-74, 102n.20, 104n.42, 125-26n.33
Syro-Palestine, 17, 18, 71-74, 77
tapeinōs, 38-42, 44, 108n.3, 113-14nn.12, 114n.15
Taylor, Greer N., 118n.16
Theissen, Gerd, 3, 36, 107n.19, 129n.32
Travis, Arthur E., 124n.105

Tristram, Henry G., 45
Troeltsch, Ernst, 20
urban-rural divisions, 22-23, 26
usury, 64
de Vaux, Roland, 109n.6
violence, revolutionary, 91-98
Vitringa, Campegius, 56
wages, 85, 91, 98. *See also* landlord ownership
Ward, Roland A., 115n.30, 121n.67
Ward, Roy Bowen, 56
White, Jr., William, 16
Wilde, James, 3, 101n.17
Wilson, Bryan, 3
Wisdom literature. *See* sapiential writings
Zahn, Theodor, 125n.14
Zealots, 23, 90, 92